Multiculturalism and Diasporic Dilemmas

The Fiction of Kamala Markandaya

Multiculturalism and Diasporic Dilemmas

The Fiction of Kamala Markandaya

Gauri Shankar Jha

ADHYAYAN

ADHYAYAN PUBLISHERS & DISTRIBUTORS

New Delhi-110002

Published by
ADHYAYAN PUBLISHERS & DISTRIBUTORS
4378/4B, 105, J.M.D. House, Murari Lal Street
Ansari Road Darya Ganj, New Delhi - 110002
Ph.: 011-23263018, 011-23277156, Fax: 23280028
Email: adhyayanpublishers@yahoo.com

Multiculturalism and Diasporic Dilemmas
The Fiction of Kamala Markandaya

Edition 2011
ISBN 978-81-8435-271-9

Printed in India

Published by Harish Chandra Yadav for Adhyayan Publishers & Distributors, Delhi. Laser Typesetting at Jain Computers and Printed at Tarun Offset Printers, Delhi

Dedicated
To
My
Gurudev
Family
and
Friends

Acknowledgements

I am deeply indebted to the Publisher Shri Harish Chandra Yadav of Adhyayan Publishers, New Delhi, who agreed, without condition, to publish the work immediately. Moreover, I cannot forget the help and cooperation that I got from my family members and friends to complete my work.

Gauri Shankar Jha

Preface

Multiculturalism has become the culture of the day particularly that of the diaspora world, though we hesitate to delete the prefix 'multi' and we are reluctant to use the term 'culture' as a common/uniform term for the entire globe as a common global culture irrespective of our meandering approval of the same. If we survey the Indian diaspora writings of the last fifty years we find abundance of instances that reflect upon the impression that the definition of culture has undergone a sea change and the present state of affairs is a uniform discipline that was earlier termed as *chatnification* or *khichrification,* mistakenly called communal, ethnic, fanatic, fundamental, alien, strange, the other, the subaltern, the oppressed, the suppressed, the downtrodden, the ruling, the class, the caste, the regional, the religious, the sectarian, the divisive -- all derogatory terms, most often used to deprecate the social fabric. The present study confines its locale of study to the Indian Diaspora women writers to diagnose the culture that develops out of contact, of the indigenous and the alien, and the consequences that most likely brings about confrontation and reluctance of different sorts, a crisis of acceptability, and so on.

Culture has played a significant role in the making of bulk of Indian Writing in English. There is an assortment of writers to provide evidence for their dexterity and aptitude in this sphere. On the other hand, Kamala Markandaya believes in the fictive exploration of the human self in the context of complex cultural values as she nurtures a complex vision of human life. As an Indian Diaspora woman writer she excels because of her ample exposure to the duel culture. We do not have an autobiography and hence we have to bank on biography, diary and collection of letters though a piece of art is to be judged as it is. However, every major novelist draws heavily upon her/his own life experiences. Kamala Markandaya and her theme of themes of uprootedness, racial tensions and prejudice, conflict between tradition and materialism, faith and reason, primitivism and technology, a search for one's true self, the experience of exile and alienation, with a string of autobiography—the conflict between the Eastern and the Western values, and the cultural dualism. Different kinds of responses to the situation of cultural multiplicity may be diagnosed. Kamala Markandaya steers clear of all "isms" and "ologies", chiefly concerned with presenting a slice of life, however, we view her "slice" with reference to the characters she has created; we feel it is not a slice of living reality but something tinned and preserved for a pretty long time, most often her female characters seem to be artificial and contrived.

Gauri Shankar Jha

Contents

1

Multiculturalism and Kamala Markandaya

Multiculturalism has become the culture of the day particularly that of the diaspora world, though we hesitate to delete the prefix 'multi' and we are reluctant to use the term 'culture' as a common/uniform term for the entire globe as a common global culture irrespective of our meandering approval of the same. If we survey the Indian diaspora writings of the last fifty years we find abundance of instances that reflect upon the impression that the definition of culture has undergone a sea change and the present state of affairs is a uniform discipline that was earlier termed as *chatnification* or *khichrification* mistakenly called communal, ethnic, fanatic, fundamental, alien, strange, the other, the subaltern, the oppressed, the suppressed, the downtrodden, the ruling, the class, the caste, the regional, the religious, the sectarian, the divisive - all derogatory terms, most often used to deprecate the social fabric. The present study confines its locale of study to the Indian Diaspora women writers to diagnose the culture that develops out of contact, of the indigenous and the alien, and the consequences that most

---

* To begin with I wish to make it clear at the very outset that I address "Indian Diaspora Women Writers" as "Her"

likely brings about confrontation and reluctance of different sorts, a crisis of acceptability, and so on.

Culture has played a significant role in the making of bulk of Indian Writing in English. There is an assortment of writers to provide evidence for their dexterity and aptitude in this sphere. We may begin with the pillars of Indian English Writing, which are Mulk Raj Anand, Raja Rao and R.K. Narayan. Anand and his Western orientation becomes clear from his concept of nature, time and man's relation to man. His heroes, Munoo - the coollie, Bakha the untouchable, Bhikhu - the chamar, Lal Singh - the peasant have indomitable spirit; his protagonists do not have typical traditional fatalism; for him Man is the measure of everything, "the dreamer of all dreams, hopping up towards Shelly's golden millennium, he sings like Whitman the song of himself and of all".(Prasad, 1983,16) His young heroes look towards a more perfect future; and above all, he believes in the intrinsic value of every individual irrespective of his caste, class, and other affiliations. In Anand's novels cultural dualism finds adequate expression through the combination of European Hellenism with Indian social consciousness. Metaphysical stance has been forged by Raja Rao which transcends the material scientific Western civilization taking cues from the Upanishadic tradition and Indian philosophy. His **The Serpent and the Rope** sublimates various experiences into a vision of life. It is a potent response to the promise or threat of cultural collision. In fact, the kindred consciousness of the East and the West impinges upon Ramaswamy's character. The twain is contrasted both in external setting and internal mental landscape. The Western world is perceived in tender, poetic and spiritual terms: the white roads in France go to the infinity of the three seas; Paris becomes an area of oneself; the Thames is the river that lives on dreams and dreams. The novelist finds Indian parallels in the Western land. The marriage between Madeline and Ramaswamy does not sustain primarily because the ethos of two different cultures resist merging into each other. Raja Rao believes in irrevocability of one's Dharma. The novelist is obviously in favour of India, of Hinduism, but he does not denigrate the heritage of another. He believes that the integrity lies in being true to one's own background. In a sense, the implication of the novel is that one has to be true to one's culture to find one's true self. Cultural dualism shapes Raja Rao's consciousness to a significant extent. We find a few writers for whom the confrontation does not result in any tension, creative or otherwise. They write with a conviction that the acquired value alone can sustain their views of lives; the best example is D.K Karaka who has written novels such as **Just Flesh, There Lay the City,** and **We Never Die** set in England with British characters displaying the author's knowledge of English life and culture. However, it makes no contribution either to English or Indian Literature because it fails to embody realities, and are mere facile attempts. There is another group of novelists for whom the inter-cultural tension exists but does not seriously affect the course of events in their fictional world, for example, R.K. Narayan and K. Nagarajan with their works **Malgudi** and **Kedaram** which may be taken as the microcosm of the macrocosm without any obvious or palpable framework of alien culture. O.P. Mathur has written an article *"The West Wind Flows Through Malgudi"* (Mathur, 1984, 27-37) where he explicates a consistent awareness of the Western culture, yet Narayan is a novelist weaving his tapestry out of his own cotton and wool. This is reflected in Narayan's depiction of characters; his women characters remind us of our next-door neighbours, of extremely familiar women whom we know in a multiplicity of roles. The third and the most significant group comprise all those novelists who have tried to locate various consequences of the encounter between indigenous Indian culture and the Western scientific materialism in his sensibility, for instance, Anand makes his stance clear in his novels: "He is a rational humanist in the Western tradition, believing in the power of science to improve material conditions, in progress and in the quality of all men, and his manifest intention is to propagate his beliefs through his novels". (Mukherjee, 1971, 75)

On the other hand, Kamala Markandaya believes in the fictive exploration of the human self in the context of complex cultural values as she nurtures a complex vision of human life. As an Indian Diaspora woman writer she excels because of her ample exposure to the duel culture. We do not have an autobiography and hence we have to bank on biography, diary and collection of letters though a piece of art is to be judged as it is. However every major novelist draws heavily upon her/his own life experiences. D. H. Lawrence aptly observes that, "The author never escapes from himself; he pads along the vicious circle of himself. There is hardly a writer who gets out of the vicious circle of himself or a painter of either". (Heinemann, 1961, 180) American novelist, Irving Wallace, observes, "Whether any character has ever been or could ever be entirely imaginary is still debatable". (Wallace, 1967, 11) In fact no fictional character or episode can be fully imaginary in abstraction for the simple reason that imagination is the direct product of reality. Helen Hull, a psychologist aptly notes," Imagination is the faculty of rearranging the known, of transmitting it into something new".(Wallace,1967,12) Obviously, the novel draws it sustenance inevitably from the life of the novelist as well as from the creative power of imagination, and so is the case of Kamala Markandaya and her theme of themes of uprootedness, racial tensions and prejudice, conflict between tradition and materialism, faith and reason, primitivism and technology, a search for one's true self, the experience of exile and alienation, with a string of autobiography—the conflict between the Eastern and the Western values, and the cultural dualism. Different kinds of responses to the situation of cultural multiplicity may be diagnosed. Kamala Markandaya steers clear of all "isms" and "ologies", chiefly concerned with presenting a slice of life, however, we view her "slice" with reference to characters she has created we feel it is not a slice of living reality but something tinned and preserved for a pretty long time, most often her female characters seem to be artificial and contrived. Nayantara Sehgal vindicates the duality of awareness mostly through man-woman relationship. Her women characters, by and large, are hurt individuals seeking fulfilment even outside marriage. In **A Time to be Happy**, Meera and Rashmi, the mother and the daughter swing to tradition and change or to native and alien culture. In **The Day in Shadow**, there is an attempt at a synthesis through the union of Simrit and Raj where we find a meaning in assimilation without loss to native heritage. Anita Desai shows her tangible concern with the multicultural situation only in her novel **Bye-Bye Blackbird**. In Desai's novels the acuteness of dilemma is lost in welter of lyricism and her characters who look like tinsels of loose sentiments or readymade ideas, hardly come out as round figures. Ruth Jhabvala, herself a foreigner, lived in India for long, and thus has probed the encounter of two cultures. But reading her novels one feels that she is an outsider floating on the fringe of essential India rather than cutting into its depth. She approaches her women characters rather awkwardly which betrays a lack of understandings. Nayantara Sahgal, Anita Desai and Jhabvala have explored only one dimension of this impinging reality in their novels. Kamala Markandaya is the only woman novelist who has fully explored and delineated, in terms of situation and character, the realities of characters, especially of women, caught in a conflict of cultures. Her fit ion captures the multiple dimensions of cultural encounter. Conflict, assimilation, acculturation and deculturation - all the possibilities resulting from an interaction of two cultures are perceived with candour and intensity in her novels. ***Nectar in a Sieve, A Handful of Rice*** and ***Two Virgins*** bear formative influences of the Western culture on Indian life, but other novels are complete metaphors of Indian life and reality shaped by the operative cultural dualism in her consciousness. Women who remain rooted in the Indian ethos do not respond to westernization with ease. By and large they come out as defected characters.

A tragic tale, **Nectar in a Sieve** is that of the agony and suffering of a peasant couple, Nathan and Rukmani, of a South Indian Village. Through their contact with the

English medical missionary Dr. Kensington, affectionately called 'Kenny' by villagers, the author brings out the opposite view-point of simple and fatalist creature of the soil. The peasants endure their miseries with calm resignation. The enlightened Englishman nourished on ideals of liberalism, is both surprised and shocked to see it and commits himself to the welfare of these innocent villagers. Talking to Rukmani he remarks at one point that he does not know which his country is. Though at times heis annoyed with the inscrutable ways of Indian peasant, he never turns out to be a member of the oppressive ruling community. He is a kind-hearted sympathetic character. His presence haunts the novel from beginning to the end and like the chorus in the Greek drama he is both a participant and a natural observer in the action of the novel. Through the character of Kenny, his ideas and his services and his attitudes, Markandays produces an objective attitude of India. However, the principal character in an intense drama of '**Nectar in a Sieve**' is women. Kamala Markandaya speaks of her agony and travails.

Some Inner Fury has many dimensions. The author highlights in the novel two prominent aspects of India's confrontation with Britain, the impact of Western education and civilization on the outlook of Indians, and the conflict between India and Britain arising from the latter's politician dominance over the former. The novel has a variety of characters representing Western culture, Indian culture, those who hate each other and also characters that assimilate the qualities of both cultures. The novel has political dimension; it is an exploration into personal relationship of characters belonging to two different races. The traits of political theme and the story of love-relationship intermingle into the Quit India Movement or Struggle for Independence. The beauty of the novel lies in unifying the various planes of experiences, emerging from the co-existence of two cultures. The overall impression that one gathers is that Markandays's female characters like the Indian earth do not change or are extremely slow in registering change.

A Silence of Desire is juxtaposition between spiritual

faith and materialism. The crisis in the life of Dandekar whose wife Sarojini goes to seek faith cur for her tumor from a Swami is the crisis resulting from a clash between Indian spiritual faith and relation modernism emerging from a contact with the Western culture. The character of Swami remains mysterious and the situation also is not fully resolved but the tension constitutes the vital experience of the novel. **Possession** enacts further dimensions of conflict between Indian spiritualism and Western materialism. This novel may be described as an allegory of the direction the independent India has to follow on its onward march to its progress. In the story of Valmiki and Caroline the novel suggests that India has to draw substance from life giving springs of its own culture. Valmiki is a rustic Indian artist; he is a symbol of the raw Independent India, for the possession of whose soul Caroline Bell symbolizing the Western civilization, makes an all out effort. Alienated from the spiritual roots of the country, Val's artistic talents wither and smoother. His final return to the Swami is suggestive of the reality that while a brief contact with the Western culture is useful, finally India's fulfilment lies in its own nourishing spiritual power. The spiritual side of India is imaged in the women like Rukmani. The Western woman is her opposite. They represent materialism and sensuality of the West. Caroline is the very opposite of Rukmani.

Cultural dualism is transmuted in **The Coffer Dams** into a conflict between technological power and the forces of nature and primitive living. This is more ambitious novel and here the novelist jostles a throng of British Indian characters into cross cultural situations, ways of life and attitude of mind. Clinton is the typical representative of European technological civilization who looks upon India as the vast sprawling enigma. He represents the ruthless efficiency of business minded British engineers. The chief of the tribe symbolizes suffering and tension as well as underlying hope and faith of uprooted inhabitants of the hills. However, Helen and Bashiam symbolize the forces of moderation and human attitudes. Helen gets peace and fulfilment when he experiences her union with Bashiam. For the first time she gets in her life a sense of belonging and a sense of universal inclusiveness. Helen and Bashiam represent blends of culture and the indispensable human links. This novel gives a wider backdrop to the theme of cultural encounter because here Helen, a British character, is seeking fulfilment and her true identity in an alien culture.

The Nowhere Man deals with the cultural dualism which emerges through still another dimension of human reality. Like Anita Desai's **Bye-Bye Blackbird** it is the story of Indian immigrants. Srinivas and his family make an island India on English soil. Vasantha, his wife, is Indian in essence. Her sandalwood box and the Ganges water which are immersed with her ashes in the Thames River become a cultural metaphor. Srinivas has settled in England and he tries to assimilate the acquired culture into his life. But finally he becomes a victim of racism. Both the hater and the hated are finished. The alien remains the alien. The novel takes a deeper plunge into human reality. It is a novel configuration the need for racial integration, cross cultural understanding and a cosmopolitan outlook in order that man survives as a human being in the contemporary existential chaos. In fact, **The Nowhere Man** reflects a more contemporary awareness of Kamala Markandaya's then her earlier novels had done. **The Nowhere Man** can be compared with the novels of Anita Desai and Arun Joshi or the fiction of the Western writers like Camus, Kafka, Malamud and other existentialist novelists. Like their fiction **The Nowhere Man** in its final evaluation is a fable on human isolation.

Her other novels like **A Handful of Rice, Two Virgins, The Golden Honeycomb** and **Pleasure City** do also present women playing many roles. **A Handful of Rice** implies in an indirect manner the influence of Western culture in the contrast of the locale between the village and the city. The strives of the city life, the evils of the underworld and the anger and protest of Ravi indicate the existence and awareness of Western values in Indian society caught in the crucible of change. **Two Virgins** spell out this tension in the character of the liberated Lalitha who runs away from the village, and falls prey to the lures of the film world and its ethics which represent the materialistic aspect of the Western culture. In her refusal to come to the placid and traditional fold of the village life, we find the helplessness of a character who believes so much in the purity a goodness of traditional native culture that she cannot return to it with a sullied self and at the same time she is a girl of the new spirit who belongs to the ambitious arena of the city: "She couldn't face going back to the village, it stifled her, her talents, her ambition. She intended to stay in the city where she belonged. She could look after herself." In fact Lalitha, "the liberated women" of Kamala Mrkandaya could not look after herself. He is no more than a chip of the old block. For all her fascination for films and city life she is a victim. And in this she is a sad *representative of the Indian women who irrespective of the role in which she is cast, is a victim.* **The Golden Honeycomb** also catches the princely India rooted in loyalty to the British empire and the emerging modern democratic spirit that comes as a challenge to the old rule of exploitation and a heraldic of new social, economic and cultural values. History is used as the bedrock of events and the relationship between the British and the Indian princes and the resultant complexities, Markandaya shows her awareness of complex cultural values and the development of individual consciousness. **Pleasure City,** like **The Coffer Dams,** deals with the theme of the encroachment of the Western technology on remote parts of the Indian subcontinent. In the juxtaposition between technology and primitivism and in Tully-Rikkirelationship, Markandaya once again dives deep into interracial and inter-cultural reality. Somehow women do not come out as characters that can effect change.

Of course, Purnaiah Taylor believes that if Jhabala is an outsider-insider, Kamala Markandaya is an inside-outsider in that she is an expatriate, who has been living in England for a number of years. Markandaya's fiction evinces a much broader range and offers a great variety of setting, character and effect, though her quintessential themes are equally few- viz., the East-West encounter, and woman in different life - roles. The East-West encounter takes two forms - first, a direct relationship between Indian and British characters; and secondly, the impact of the modern urban culture brought in by the British rule of traditional Indian life. Markandays's first novel, **Nectar in a Sieve** (1954) illustrates all these preoccupations. The narrator, who is also the central figure, is Rukmani, a rustic woman. The story of her hard peasant life illustrates the truth of Coleridge's Line, 'work without hope draws nectar in a sieve'. The vagaries of nature and the depredations of modern industrialism (in the shape of a tannery) force Rukmani and her husband to migrate to a city where they are fleeced. Kensington, the kind-hearted itinerant British doctor and social worker represents the better side of the West. The novel, **A Book of the Month Club** selection, has been compared to **Good Earth** by some foreign reviewers. Those who know their Indian village will, however, not fail to notice how contrived a picture of rustle lie it offers. And when the novelist proceeds to describe the public naming ceremony of Ira's child which is born in sin, one is convinced that Rukmani's village exists only in the expatriate imagination of her creator. Surely, no traditional Indian village will allow so permissive a code of sexual morality. **Some Inner Fury** (1955) and **Possession** (1963) concentrate on Indo-British personal relationships. In the former, the love of Mira for Richard is denied fruition by the fury of the Freedom Movement which tears the lovers apart. The unhappy marriage of Kitsamy, the England returned Civil Servant and Premala, his traditional Hindu wife, shows another facet of the East-West relationship. Since Richard remains a paste-board figure, the novel fails to be a tragedy of star-crossed love. An even greater air of unreality hangs over **Possession**, the story of the clash between lady Caroline and a Swami for the 'possession' of the soul of Valmiki, the rustic artist, who is lured to England by her, but later returns to his mentor. Since the Swami is also an obvious a fake, the conflict is not even adequately realized in personal terms, let alone the possibility of a larger symbolic dimension.

She subjects her theme to a far deeper probing that she is able to create living character in meaningful dilemmas. The first novel in which this is achieved is ***A Silence of Desire*** (1960). Here, the clash between the Western-oriented rationalism of Dandekar, who wants his wife Sarojini to get her operated for a tumour and the traditional religious faith of Sarojini, which relies absolutely on the faith-healing of the Swami (a much more credible figure than his counterpart *in* **Possession**) is adequately realized. It also leads to a larger conflict, exemplifying the Hegelian concept of two kinds of good pitted against each other - in this case, the domestic peace of the partially privileged middle-class represented by Dandekar versus the interests of the totally unprivileged poor who will starve if the Swami is driven away, as Dandekar and others similarly situated wish.

The superficialities in **A Handful of Rice** (1966) is quite obvious. This story of Ravi, an urban vagabond on who lowers middle-class respectability is thrust, when he marries Nalini the daughter of a poor tailor, is unconvincing because the hero's gangster friends are totally unrealized creations, while Nalini remains the typical, long-suffering Hindu wife. **The Coffer Dams** (1969) may be taken as a distinct watershed in the development of Markandaya's fiction. There is now a serious attempt to consolidate the artistic gains made in **A Silence of Desire**, at the same time the novelist also tries to evolve a new style, which sounds like a mixture of Faulkner and the later Henry James. In this narrative of the arrival of a firm of British engineers to construct a river-dam in Independent India, Markandaya offers one of her most comprehensive pictures of the Indo-British encounter. The various British attitudes to India include Clinton's studied neutrality based on the desirability of a purely working relationship with Indians; his wife Helen's curiosity and fascination for the tribals, which results in her affair with Bashiam, the 'jungly wallah'; Millie's pathological fear of the 'natives'; and Lefebvre's friendly stance. The novelist views the Indian responses in an equally objective manner, highlighting the ultra-sensitiveness of Krishnan and Gopal Rao and investing the death of the old tribal chief which coincides with the completion of the dam with obvious symbolic significance. The new style with its primacy of oblique and convoluted expression, tortured syntax and jerky sentence-structure, however, does not make for easy reading.

The Nowhere Man (1972) centres on the same theme in a more limited, but far more intensive manner, and against an English setting. Srinivas, an old Indian widower and a Londoner for the major part of his life, finds a kindred soul in old Mrs. Pickering, a divorcee. But during the anti-immigrant wave of the sixties, he is persecuted, though he does have some sympathetic white neighbours. He dies when a fanatic sets fire to his house, but even before that his discovery that he has developed leprosy (an evocative symbol both of his isolation and his disintegration) has already spelt tragedy. Unfortunately, Mrs. Pickering remains a shadowy character and the Mandarin style which continues 'to stall, to deal in obliquities' is a constant irritant.

Two Virgins (1973), a slight work of Markandaya lapses into her earlier superficiality in once again telling an unconvincing tale of Indian village life. The contrast between the two sisters, Lalitha, the 'child of grace', who yearns to become a 'town miss' and Saroja, the 'child of the soil' and the 'country miss' is utterly machine-made, while the theme of the adolescent's loss of innocence could not perhaps be handled more crudely than here.

Mrkandaya's, **The Golden Honeycomb** (1977) is her first attempt at historical fiction, the longest and the most ambitious work. This is a chronicle of three generations of the princely family of Devapur, covering a period of about a century from 1850 to Independence. The novelist appears to have too many irons in the fictional fire here. Scenes like the elaborate account of the Delhi Durbar of 1903 are in the manner of conventional historical fiction; while at many places the impression is created that what the novelist is primarily interested in is the psychological workings of the minds of the characters, irrespective of the historical setting. And along with scenes of authentic local colour, there are incidents like prince Ravi's affair with a slum-girl in Bombay, which are credible only as fantasy. The upshot is a honeycomb from the queen of a purposive centre is mission. Furthermore, the experiments of narrating the story in snippets instead of chapters and putting a major part of the narrative in the present tense are of doubtful value, considering the vast period of time covered, while the ghosts of Faulkner and James still continue to haunt the style.

Kamala Markandaya has the ability to reach down to the roots of the reality she happens to be dramatizing in a particular novel. This failure becomes more lamentable when we realize how she is wide off the mark in her depiction of female characters. How can woman give such superficial portraits of women? To the extent Kamala Markandaya presents the fight or dogged perseverance of a Rukmani she is convincing but in depicting a Lalitha or Caroline or even the slum-girl who is courted Prince Ravi, Markandays is merely creating fictional types who are neither real nor realistic. For all the influence of James deep interpretation of human character does not seem to be the domain of Kamala Markandaya. The Markandaya woman in none of her several roles seem to be central concern to their creator. They are also not quite convincing in the various roles in which they have been cast. Perhaps the experience that made a deep impression on the mind of Kamala Markandaya is her own expatriation and contact with an alien culture. The pertinent queries that follow are:

(i) What happens, to the traditional men/women, (deeply rooted in the history and culture of India,) when faced with the task of embracing an alien way of life.

(ii) Do these men/women eschew the old and embrace the new?

(iii) Is culture-shock the most crucial experience in the life of these men/women?

The burdens of the chapters that follow consist of Kamala Markandaya's men/women coming out as creative expressions of an important segment of her fiction.

REFRERENCES

1. Heinemann, W., *The Prometheus Papers of D .H. Lawrence*, London, Phoenix, 1961.
2. Mukherjee, M, *The Twice Born Fiction: Themes and Techniques of the Indian Novel in English*, Arnold-Heinemann, New Delhi., 1971.
3. Prasad, H.M, *Responses: Recent Revelations of Indian Fiction in English*, P. B. D. Bareilly, 1983.
4. Ram, A., Ed, *Perspectives on R .K .Narayan, Mathur, O.P., The West Wind Blows Through Malgudi*, Vimal Prakashan, Ghaziabad. 1984.
5. Wallace, I, *The Fabulous Originals*, Four Square Books, London. 1967.

2

Models and Metaphors of Life in Kamala's Fiction

Kamala Markandaya's fiction, when analysed minutely, brings home the truth that she does not show a sociologist's or feminist's preoccupation with women. Women constitute an important presence on the canvas of her art. Lord David Cecil makes a perceptive observation on the nature of the creative art while commenting on Jane Austen:

> A work of art is born of the union of the artist' experience and his imagination. But only certain aspects of his experience stir a deep enough response in her personality to generate his imaginative spark: only when it is inspired by them does his work have artistic lie. It is his first obligation to choose themes within the range of this experience.(Cecil,1960,100)

Jane Austen is admired by Lord Cecil for the fact that she remains within the confines of her chosen orbit. Markandaya creates her designs, as it were, on a small piece of ivory. As a painter of the Indian scene she gives intimate pictures of the Indian women. From Rukmani in **Nectar in a Sieve** to Helen in **The Coffer Dams,** or the sweet and benign Mrs. Fletcher of **Pleasure City**, Kamala Markandaya presents the kaleidoscopic view of women characters. But

Kamala Mrkandaya's central concern is not the lot of Indian women.

In fact the role played by Markandya's women is peripheral or contextual rather than central or pivotal. In Indian life woman's place is ambivalent. They are worshipped as the mother or shakti or Goddess, they are also bought, sold and burnt. No Indo-Anglian writer, not even the women like Markandaya and Kamala Markandaya are as deeply concerned with women as some great Indian writers writing in Hindi and other major Indian languages. For example Premchand, Tagoer and Sarat Chadra have written with great feeling about the suffering and glory of Indian women. Women who had remained draped in purdah or concealed in the seclusion of discreetly hidden balconies came out in the open as the wind of change began to blow in the shape of India's call for national independence. Kamala Markandaya is a product of the same phase of awakening. But she is not much concerned with women who did not literally have "a room of their own" and who in this woman-worshipping land - the haloed mother land - were denied the opportunity to live like a human being. In 1930 feminism in Europe had lost some of it edge because of the changes in women's status ushered in by great social and cultural factors. E.M. Forster dubs Virgina Woolf's feminism "old fashioned". According to Forster, "By the 1930" she had much less to complain of and seems to keep on grumbling from habit". (Forster, 1971, 14)

Even after Independence, the Indian women were still in chains, and as Kamala Markandaya had no cause for being complacent or indifferent. Except for a microscopic minority who may be described as emancipated women and who are no more than the froth on the surface of vast dormant see the mass of Indian women continued to be where they had been for centuries. To Kamala Markandaya as also to Shanta Rama Rao, Anita Desai and others the woman theme is not important either in its sociological aspect or in its creative aspect. Nevertheless, even by not noticing the women the writers speak volumes on the women question that is, in India where women are worshipped they are of no consequence in real life. But it would be wrong to infer that Kamala Markandaya is silent on the woman question. In not giving a very exalted place to women she is only being realistic about Indian life. Our myths and legends paint the ideal; our fiction reproduces the reality. "Sita" and "Shakti" belong to our myths, and Rukmani and Sarojini belong to our real life. She paints the place and plight of women in a predominantly male world. Generally it is Nathan's story, and the heroic and tragic saga of Rukmani's sacrifice gore unnoticed. By not giving them exaggerated importance Kamala Markandaya is merely writing the Indian story. Her novels present women in their many roles: Rukmani and Anasuya representing rural India, Mira, representing the educated women; Granny and Aunt Alemelu, representing the ancient tradition, and Caroline and Helen representing women who belong to an alien culture. In her rich portrait-gallery there are many faces, young, old, bright and sad. Through her women characters Kamala Markandaya has expressed the social attitudes. A widow is a bad omen; a childless woman is also a bad omen. The ideal character is the Sita-Savitry type; the suffering woman, the sacrificing woman. Almost all women characters of Kamala Markandaya conform to the stereotypes. Deep within they are Indian, and despite their education they have registered only a slight change. Even in Kamala Markandaya's world the western woman like Caroline is a temptress, a materialistic and sensual creature. The saga of the Indian woman is a saga of suffering and sacrifice, and this is what Kamala Markandaya depicts in her novels.Her range is wide but the cardinal experience is the central consciousness in all her novels. She explores the reality of living in a cultural multiplicity which is not only her personal predicament but also the compulsive national reality of India. India has been a Commonwealth country, a country which remained under British rule. Hence the interaction between the East and the West, between its own heritage and tradition and the history and development of the West have been a vital part of its own reality. In the twentieth century, the age of global cultural diffusion, no country can insulate itself against the influences from different cultures. Since the cultural interaction between India and England has been deep and extensive, most of the Indian novelists writing in English have explored this enigmatic experience of cultural multiplicity in one or other novels.

We have Balchandra Rajan, Santa Ram Rau, Raja Rao, Nayantara Sahgal, Anita Desai and Arun Joshi who have written significant and interesting novels where they have fictionalized some dimensions of this dilemma. What strikes us most obviously in the case of Kamala Markandaya is the fact that she has not dealt with the theme of East-West encounter or cultural interaction in one or two novels only. In fact, it has been her central concern, her persistent preoccupation, her flame of creative imagination right from the publication of her first novel **Nectar in a Sieve** published in 1954 to her last novel **Pleasure City** released in 1982. She has explored from varying perspectives the cultural dualism as a vital and intrinsic part of Indian life and identity. While other novelists have been concerned with one aspect of this complex problem, Kamala Markandaya tries to explicate its myriad dimensions in her different novels. In **Nectar in a Sieve, A Silence of Desire, A Handful of Rice** and **Two Virgins**, the women-theme comes up indirectly in the onslaught of industry on rural life, in the clash between the life of faith and the life of reason. Western materialistic concept of pleasure and progress pitted against the traditional Indian life-style also constitutes the theme of her novel. The tannery in **Nectar in a Sieve** is an implicit but potent symbol of the terrors of technology. It is the exclusive gift of Western culture. The tannery gets a wider form in a symbol of **The Coffer Dams** and also in the latest concept of pleasure houses in her novel **Pleasure City.** The happy Arcadian atmosphere, the hearty contentment that Rukmani feels and enjoys, the gradual destruction of innocence of the village life, the death of Nathan in the city, and the final return of Ruknmani with the leper boy do not merely constitute the tenets of rural tragedy, they also depict India caught in the dynamics of change. Though women do not play an active part in this slow process of change yet they define their stand by resisting the lure of modernity which is represented by the industrial culture of city culture. The impact of an alien culture on the Indian life is subterranean in this novel, but the reality of cultural dualism expresses itself through the character of the English doctor, his approach to Indian society and people, the neutrality of the city life and the destructive consequences of the tannery. Markandaya is not critical of either culture, she is candid and objective but we can discern a message in the novel that the strength of Indian culture lies in the spiritual stamina which finds an appropriate symbol in Rukmani.

A Silence of Desire is Markandaya's representation of the contemporary consciousness which shows a new dimension in the spiritual crisis of the couple Sarojini and Dandekar. This spiritual crisis is a problem of psychological adjustment in the life of this middle-class family. Sarojini is the image of the newly emergent middle-class traditional housewife in India. Dandekar is the voice of the newly emergent new everyman in India. In other words the novel may be described as a parable on the conflict between the Indian spiritual faith and the modernism born of India's contact with the West. Saojini seeks faith cure from tumour from a Swami but her husband asks her to go in for a scientific cure through operation. Sarojini remarks:

> Yes, you can call it healing by faith, or healing by the grace of God, if you understand what that means. But I do not expect you to understand you with your Western notions, your superior talk of ignorance and superstition when all it means is that you don't know what lies beyond reason and you prefer not to find out. (Markandaya, 1966, 63)

Such conflict between faith and reason is recurrent in Indian life. In its various manifestations it finds expression in the Granny of R.K. Narayan's **Waiting for the Mahatma** or in Kamala Markandaya's Aunt Alemelu in **Two Virgins** they suspect and resist change. Nevertheless, these ancient creatures are not treated as the dead stumps of ancient trees as old fossils. These old womenare also treated as repositories of wisdom. In the conflict between faith and reason they represent the life of faith. This is the result of the co-presence of Indian spiritual tradition and Western pragmatic outlook. Consequently Dandekar who is a product of this transition feels, "He couldn't make up his mind because heart spoke one way, head the other and sometimes the two changed places". (Markandaya,1966,14)

In the presence of the Swami he feels a greater chaos because when he was before the Swami, nothing material or physical mattered. In this dichotomy between the body and the soul, the martial and the spiritual lies the essential predicament of the modern Indian society. Thus **A Silence of Desire** poignantly recreates an important dimension of the Indian experience. Kamala Markandaya uses her women characters as sensitive barometers to register the impact of a major transition. **A Handful of Rice** shows covertly how modernism brought in by the Western influence aggravates the protest of the protagonist against the traditional environment in seeking his fulfillment by carving his career independently. Groaning under the smothering pressure of poverty and squalor Ravi leaves his village and joins the general exodus to the city and floating through the indifferent streets, lands into the underworld of the petty criminals. Prompted by his love for Nalini whom he married afterwards, he gives up the immoral ways and struggles heart and soul to carry out the responsibilities that have fallen on his holders. To Ravi who is a drifter, and who ahs drifted from a life of misery into a worse life of crime Nalini is the redeeming factor. Anchored in Nalini Ravi swings back towards life. Thus by and large women in Kamala Markandaya's novel are positive and life-sustaining. The novel comes to an end with the crowd scene where he joins the hungary mob that plunder the rice godown. But when his term comes to burl a brick at the rice row he fails to act: "But suddenly he couldn't. The strength that had inflammed him, the strength of suppressed laminated anger, ebbed as quickly as it had risen. His hand dropped". (Markandaya,1966,237) Margaret P. Joseph rightly observes that "in this dichotomy between idea and fact in the impossibility of bridging the gap between desire and honest fulfillment, lies the essence of the tragic". (Joseph,1980,62)

No doubt, the basis of the tragedy in this novel is the frightening dilemma of human conscience but we can remark with a fairness that behind the dilemma of conscience lies the truth of modernism in Indian life ensuring largely from the impact of Western culture which is pitted against traditional Indian ethical ethos. In Kamala Markandaya's fiction the family despite the drift towards the city is still intact. Like birds they migrate, cover long distances but nevertheless, when the time comes, they get together and build nests. The women play a vital role in the perennial drama of Indian life. In **Two Virgins** we often hear of the British rulers from Appa, a freedom fighter who was called a terrorist and whose house was burnt by the Tummies. He understands that it was a British strategy to divide the people and set them one against another to rule in India, yet he has no rancour against the British and other Europeans. When his wife criticizes European doctors and says that they have nothing, Appa snubs her by pointing out: "One must take an overall view. One imbibes what is bad in the West as well as what is good... there are no national frontiers"(Markandaya,1977,113)

What Appa says, is a desire to correct the lop-sidedness or imbalance in the approach of the women characters. Appa suggests a sane and realistic approach to the process of change. The older women are dogmatic. But the young ones, tempted by the glare of modernity embrace it without discrimination, and the result is the kind of fate that overtakes Lalitha. Appa is a balanced character who assimilates the Western influence into the texture of his outlook. His daughter Lalitha is portrayed as a liberated girl. She is conscious of her uncommon beauty and is also highly ambitious. Mr. Gupta, the film director who comes to the village for a documentary film, exploits her weakness and promises to give her a role in the film. She suffers in his hand. If Appa has assimilated the best part of the West, Mr. Gupta has imbibed its worst. Though Lalitha has spoilt herself, yet she refuses to come to the village and is lost in the city: "She couldn't face going back to the village: it stifled her, her talents, her ambition. She intended to stay in the city where she belonged. She could look after herself". (Markandaya, 1977, 236)

Cultural dualism shown in this novel itself through the girl's growing awareness of the adult world and of the slow but irresistible encroachment of new and material values on the ancient belief and old established relationships within the family and the village. Deep within the Kamala Markandaya woman is like Aunt Alemelu who is skeptical of change, who identifies the glitter and glare of modern civilization with perversion, degradation and misfortune.

Possession explores still another dimension of the theme of cultural interaction, in which women play significant roles. The novelist probes into the dilemma for a deeper perspective. The theme of national identity, the possessive trait of a culture, and the negative influences of an interaction between two cultures are the important tenets of experience in this novel. Here the novelist gives almost a sociological interpretation of Indian-England relationship. She gauges her understanding of two different cultures, two different ways of life through the three-cornered story of Caroline Bell, the English Woman, Valmiki, the Indian native boy and the Swami. Valmiki, the rustic Indian artist, is the symbol of raw independent India for the possession of whose soul the formidable Caroline Bell symbolizing the Western culture and civilization, makes an all-out effort. Alienated from spiritual roots of his country Valmiki's artistic talent becomes dormant. Only when Caroline establishes his contact with the Swami who is the fountain spring of sustaining Indian spiritualism, that Valmiki's talents begin to blossom again. His final return to the Swami is the return of the native. In his suffering and anguish, in his failure and inability, in his temporary inactivity Valmiki shows the malevolence of an alien culture. In her possessiveness and pride, in her passion and arrogance, in her materialism and pride, in her passion and arrogance, in her materialism and physicality Caroline is a cogent symbol of the destructive fury of the Western culture. The implied message of the novel is that while a brief contact with the West may be worthwhile, may prove to be a fertilizing element but its ultimate fulfillment is possible only through its nourishment by spiritual values. To tell the truth, the novel shows how India and England didn't really understand each other, how their political relationship stifled their cultural co-operation. The novel may be a parable of colonialism, but in its deeper implication the novel illustrates how a culture tries to destroy the life-force of another culture. A man can express one's true self and can fulfil one's being only when he plants his roots in soil of his native culture. The novel enacts this dilemma more powerfully than Rajan's **The Dark Dancer** and Nayantara Sahgal's **A Time to be Happy**. In the story of Valmiki, Kamala Markandaya shows for once that preservation of basic cultural traits are necessary for people to survive and flourish. Yet another dimension of the woman theme finds its fictional expression through the polemics of personal love and racial reality in **Some Inner Fury**. The novel explores the process of ethnic encounter through the story of Richard and Mira, Kit and Premala, Govind and Hickey. The novelist is able to pit personal love against the national movement and ethnic crisis. Richard is a symbol of the most liberal Englishman who had forgotten the decencies of England and authoritarianism of empire. "When he sits cross-legged on the floor of a Brahmin restaurant Mira bursts with pride and delight, "There is no one like Richard, no one at all like my love". (Markandaya, 1955, 106)

The relationship between these two whose love is so deep, genuine and based on mutual understanding is torn asunder by the centrifugal force of ethnic consciousness. Just after Richard escapes being hit by a bomb thrown at him, he exclaims to Mira:

> It is a terrible thing to feel unwanted. To be hated·(Markandaya,1955,137)

When Mira pleads desperately, "Richard - this feeling isn't for you. Or, or for people like you", he remarks gently:

> Do you really think people can be singled out like that? One by one, each is an individual? At a time like this after today? (Markandaya,1955,185)

Racial consciousness is the concern of the individuals. Still another dimension of cultural dualism finds a fictional correlate in the crisis of identity in Markandaya's novel **The Nowher Man.** In the story of Srinivas who has spent two third of his life in England and has come to look upon England and his own country the condition of immigration deepens into the predicament of exile and alienation. The contours of his identity are mutilated. He belongs to nowhere:I have been transformed into a stranger, and the unwanted man and examine a pair of hands whose stigmata would be the excuse.(Markandaya,1975,241)The quest for his identity indicates the necessity of cultural coexistence. Mrs. Fletcher tells Srinivas:

> There can be compensations. If one is cut off from one's culture there is always the adopted one to draw upon. (Markandaya,1975,71)

Mrs. Fletcher who is a pure Christian soul and a loving blossom of English culture tells Srinivas:

> You don't want to pay any attention to Fred. He doesn't know what he's talking about. You've got as much right to leave her as what he has. Even if you weren't born in this country, Mr. Srinivas, you belong here, and don't let anyone convince you different. (Markandaya, 1975, 174)

Mr. Srinivas dies but his death is not merely aftermath of racial hatred; it is a pointer towards the universal desire and necessity for cultural coexistence. He is a positive symbol of cultural diffusion. In **The Coffer Dams** and **Pleasure City** cultural dualism knocks out its fictional idiom through the theme of techno-economic development and its impact on the indigenous cultural value systems. Markandaya expatiates upon the East-West theme by highlighting the economic help that an underdeveloped country like India receives from England. In other words the novel explores the techno-economic development and its impact on the indigenous cultural value system. She has earlier dealt with certain aspects of it in a straightforward rural setting in **Nectar in a Sieve**. Fifteen years later, Markandaya's creative powers find a mature expression in an imaginative rendering of the trials and tribulations of a tribe, struggling for survival in face of an irresistible technological Juggernaut, doggedly pushed by a team of efficient engineers over their Indian assistants.

We find in **Pleasure City** a more contemporary form of the East-West interaction. The dam was a necessity for the development of the country, the pleasure city is a luxury complex. Here is also enough possibility for a dramatization of the ethical, aesthetic and cultural values of Indians and Europeans. This latest novel indicate a direction as it were toward the possibility of coexistence and assimilation of cultures. In the character of Tully, Markandaya forges out a symbol for future possibilities. Even if he departs, even if he holds on to his own ways, even if he is a true Englishman, he is as human as the native living on the sea-coast. His participation in life with Rikki, his sharing of the world around and his warm relationship with him extend further the symbolic dimensions of the characters like Doctor Keny, Richard, Helen and Mrs. Picketing. They are the living metaphors of European culture and their relationship with Rukmani, Mira, Srinivas, Bashiam and Rikkim who are the finest blossoms of Indian culture, is an exploration of the true identity of our country. The true predicament of our country is continuity and change, tradition and modernity, rural richness and technological triumphs, ethical values and existential pressure, spiritual faith and skeptical intellect.

And all these find expression chiefly in the attitudes of the women characters.

Kamala's preoccupation with women, young, old, rural, urban, Indian and the European enables her to explore. Indian society in all its myriad prismatic shades. It also imparts her novels depth and symbolic richness. In the modern times novel is not merely a means of realistic presentation of the life around or an entertaining division; it has become a serious mode of exploring man's dilemma, sociological, psychological, existential and metaphysical. Almost all his novels have deeper implications. **Nectar in a Sieve** has a tragic appeal. Rukmani is a heroic figure reminiscent of Hardy's Henchard who claimed that his sufferings were not greater than he could endure or the old man of Hemingway who persist and prevails. In fact, **Nectar in a Sieve** is a work in the tradition of tragedies exploring the riddle of human existence through human suffering, finally leaving the reader with a deepened awareness of human life. **Some Inner Fury**, a tragedy engendered by the historically important Independence Movement exalts personal love beyond race and colour. **A Silence of Desire** enacts the dilemma of the transitory phase of the nation, the polemic of tradition and modernity, faith and scepticism but the novelist's real achievement lies in "the projection of this theme through the awakening of a mind developing from thoughtless complacency to tremulous introspection.(Joseph,1980,153) **A Handful of Rice**, a work depicting the general exodus of the poor people to the town, comes up as a novel on the existential dilemma of the modern Indian who cannot shed his ethical heritage. **The Coffer Dams** explores racial interaction but the novel also becomes a drama of quest. Helen is in quest of fullness of life. Fullness of life is always related to the cultural context we live in. Paul Kurtz speaks of happiness in the sense of fullness of being. That is what Helen seeks: "a life in which qualities of satisfaction and excellence are present".(Kurtz,1974,100)

He mentions importance of love, enlisting certain necessities for a full life, to live authentically, the need to discharge surplus energy, a generalized sense of community, 'to broaden horizons to belong', the need to love one's self and 'creative actualization', the need to bring into function one's potentialities. Kurtz adds: "The injunction is to be myself, not what others would have one be; I must express my own nature in all its variety and create something new". (Kurtz,1974,102) Helen moves out in the need for self-affirmation and tries to achieve the sense of a full life by living not for public approval, but to live authentically. **The Nowhere Man**, a novel on ethnic encounter, finally emerges as an allegory of loneliness. The existential alienation sublimates in a spiritual condition of mind. With his only son getting away from them, the Srinivas couple start the "Vanaprastha Dharma". But they are not spiritually strong enough to get out of the bonds and devote the time in contemplating upon the final release. The loneliness forced upon Srinivas helps him to some extent to alleviate a disposition that has some elements of *Sanvas Ashram* which is symbolically inaugurated by his wearing the *dhoti* and giving up his usual cumbrous dress. One day at the height of racial hatred when he finds on his doorstep excrement, he cleans up the place himself. In another day a dead mouse is found on his doorstep. He picks it up very patiently carries it away and burns it. He has reached a stage when nothing is disgusting to him and no work is mean. He looks upon the hats of Fred and the warmth of Mr. Field alike; he has ever the magnanimity to condone Frad's criminality. The **Gita** speaks of such a state as **Yoga**. He shows that the **Gita** would describe the highest mark of culture in his sympathy for his fellow beings, comparing theirs with his own forlorn state. The loneliness of others can be appreciated by him because he is himself lonely. Srinivas is grilled by adversity and passes through a lifelong suffering and pain, a modification that has melted away all the dross in his character. He even passes through the ordeal of fire at the end but comes out of it unscathed, because he does not die to burns. He has the equanimity to recognize constable Kent just before his death and dies calmly as though he has folded up his self.

There is a positive movement towards assimilation in **Pleasure City**. Tension in togetherness is prominent in **Possession.** In **Some Inner Fury** Richard and Marlowe, in **The Coffer Dams,** Helen and Bashim, in **The Nowhere Man,** Srinivas and Mr. Pickering have obliterated racial difference. They have departed, but they have forged their ways towards cultural co-existence. Tully and Rikki also depart but the twilight of togetherness is now in sight:

> There was a faint light visible, a pearly sheen on distant horizon. The false dawn, they called it, forerunner of dawn proper.(Markandaya,1982,341)

It is the Indian writer's inability to paint a picture of women she had been by and large invisible in public life. Their dominant role in myths and legends and their total absence from the theater of real life suggests a break with the past. It also suggests the difficult predicament of the Indian written engaged in writing novel. Indo-Anglian fiction was the inevitable outcome of the Indian exposure to Western culture and art forms like the novel. As Indo-Anglian fiction had a late start, a diffident and doubtful early life and was many a times made up and meant for the Western reader, the women characters who can be said to be real and clear, strong and convincing appear much later and paler than in the novels in the regional languages. In the early novels, Indian as well as Indo-Anglian and Anglo-Indian, the women are too distant from reality, too crude, moralized or sentimentalized. But in the Indian languages, the writers quickly turned towards reality and Anglo-Indian fiction was almost forgotten except for a few writers like Kipling. Indo-Anglian fiction, however, went on giving romanticized images of women, and in general was unable to grapple with reality for quit a long time. That is why professor V.G. Gokak dubbed this genre of fiction as 'a hot-house plant' 'a Shakuntala in skirts' 'born by a Caesarian operation' (Gokak, 1960, 52-53)While Iyengar called it a 'singular offspring' and wondered whether this was 'legitimate or illegitimate' born when 'England and India had come together'.(Iyenger,1969,4)

The reasons for the inability of Indo-Anglian fiction to effect reality in its initial stages may be traced to the difficulties the writers had to face. They were writing in an acquired language. The double difficulty of giving expression and transmuting the experience in English is recognized by Dr. Meenakshi Mukherjee who has called the Indo-Anglian novel **'The Twice Born Fiction'.** (Mukherjee, 1972, title) The experience of the writer has to go through the pains of two birth to see the light of day. The problem would be even more difficult when the writers tried to deal with the uneducated Indian woman.

As we know, India has been the confluence of many cultures. The Indian woman reacted to the Western culture with avidity, took up new ideas and forms and assimilated them the fact that Indo-Anglian fiction did finally achieve some success in representing woman authentically is due to what Professor Rajan has called the 'Indian capacity for assimilation and tolerance'.(Varghese,1971,179) The writers absorbed from the East as well as from the West. The decade at the turn of the century were the days of renaissance. Indian writers fond Scott's historical romances suited to their purpose of obliquely expressing their patriotism, their religious and cultural views, without much political risk. But in the novels of Scott given to adventure and exploits, woman was just an appendage - a symbol of beauty, sweetness, purity, faithful love, as in the days of chivalry that Scott recreated. As Indian writers followed his steps, they too turned to historical romance. The woman of their own times lay neglected. This was the case in the early novels with Indian fiction writers in the Indian languages also, though they came out of this stage earlier than the Indo-Anglian fiction writers did. Early novels like **Padmini** (1909) by T. Rama Krishna, **The Prince of Destiny** (1909) by S. K.Ghosh, **Hindupur** (1909) by S.K. Mitra. **The Slave Girl of Agra** (1909) by R.C. Dutt, **Nur Jehan** (1909) by Sir Jogendra Singh, **The Unveiled Court** (1933) by U. Behadur reflect the influence of Scott and revolve around ancient glamour and glory and give an idolized image of the Indian woman culled from history and legend. The Indian novels of this also show the same trend. **Ananda Math** (1882) by Bankim Chandra Chatterjee in Bengali, or **Maisorcha Wagh** (1890) by Hari Narayan Apte in Marathi, are early examples of this trend towards historical romance. These novels were not so much concerned with reflecting the contemporary situation of the Indian woman as with the desire to create and provoke a national consciousness. But as for the image of woman as a source of power, the **Shakti,** the writers turned not to the Western source, but to their own rich heritage coming down to them from ancient times. In **Ananda Math**, for example, Bankim Chandra created the symbol of the motherland, and *'Vandemateram'* was on the lips of all patriots throughout the freedom struggle. The ancient Indian mother-image was taken up, transfused and applied to the country. That is why R.W. Frazer comments, "the novels themselves owe their form to Western influences, but the subject-matter and spirit are essentially native". And he calls Bankim Chandra, "The first great creative genius modern India has produced", for he has revealed, "the inward spirit of Indian life and thought".(Frazer,1920,89)

However, Frazer, sees more of poetic fancy, spiritual mysticism and less of objective realism in Bankim's works, and this is also true of most of the writers of historical romances. But within the sphere of patriotic-historical romance these writers did the salutary work of turning to their own ancient glorious heritage for inspiration. Bankim Chandra, for example, has combined the mother-image and the **Shakti** in **Durgeshanandini** (trans. 1890). The problems and predicament of real women could not for long be ignored by these writers when reform was in the air. The problem of the suffering Indian wife as seen in **Rajmohan's Wife** (1864). **Poison Tree** (n.d.) appearing first in Bengali, then translated in English, shows the widow and the silent suffering chaste, sacrificing Indian wife, both the types very common in Indo-Anglian as well as Indian fiction. Suraj Mukhi, the heroine, has the calm dignity, the graceful gentleness of an ideal, faithful Hindu wife, while Kamala, fated to widowhood at a young age and brought under Suraj Mukhi's protection proves to be a disturbing force in the complex of the joint family. In Krishnakanta's **Will** (n.d.), again, we see the young widow inspiring love in a young man's heart. The reason for recurrence of the Hindu widow in Indian fiction may be observed in the changing social conditions. The Sati custom had been abolished by law and reforms were trying to see that people followed the law. Child marriages were still common. There were a large number of child widows. Men could remarry, but not women. The Western rationalism and humanitarianism and the spirit of social reform prodded by patriotism turned the minds of the reformers and writers to the problem of the widow. The widow had appeared in some Anglo-Indian novels too. But the solution of remarriage and change of religion was obviously impracticable. Bankim Chandra highlights the problem and the suffering as well as the frustration of the Hindu widow in the context of Indian society.

Gradually, as writers acquired skill, they took up this problem and showed its depth. In Tagore's **Choker Bali** (1902) (trans. .**Binodini,** 1959) Indian fatalism is fully operative, throwing perverse events in Binodini's path. Her fate as a widow, without any right to love or to happiness in life acquires great intensity. As a woman she cannot help responding to her lower, but as a Hindu widow she cannot marry him. So she remains a silent, throbbing longing woman. The frustrations, yearnings and sufferings of Binodini gain in intensity because the writer keeps close to reality. In the Marathi novel, **Yamunaryatan** (1857) by Baba Padamji, the widow marries a Christian, as in **Seeta** by Taylor. The demands of reality were pressing themselves on the writers. Ready-made solutions were rejected. Hari Harayan Apte's (who also turned from writing historical romance to novel with social problems) **Pan Laxat Kon Cheto** (Marathi, **But Who Pays Attention**?) will suffice to prove the point. The realistic portrayal of widow's misery in the character of yamy opened the eyes of the Marathi readers to the fate of the widow. Sarat Chandra Chatterjee carried the torch of realism to many nooks and corners of Bengali homes and showed widows in actual surroundings. Iyenger points out how 'there is an increasingly bolder approach to the actualities of life'(Iyenger,1973,318) in the works of Bankim Chandra, Tagore and Sarat Chandre Chattarjee.

In the attempts to coordinate reality and reform in the portraiture of women can also be seen in Romesh Chander Dutt's **The Lake of Palms** (trans.1933). Its original, **Sensar,** had appeared as early as in 1885 in Bengali. A Hindu widow from a Bengali village faces suffering and poverty and dies after bringing up and marrying off her daughters. As the Western educated Sarat falls in love with Sudha, the child widow, and as she silently and secretly responds to him, there rises a hornet's nest of suspicions, fears, anger and scandal, but there is also sympathy. In the midst of all this reality the writer also offers a solution put forth by the great Indian reformers who had turned to the scriptures in their pristine purity. For older widow they recommend that they should remain faithful to the memory of their husbands. For such a child-widow as Sudha 'the scriptures distinctly sanction remarriage'.(Dutt,1933,108)

In this way, reality and reformatory seal combine in Dutt's treatment of the problem of the widow. Tagore showed the yearning of the widow; Apte saw her throbbing and then her dull misery; Taylor and Baba Padamji offered change of religion as a solution, while Dutta cleared away the cluttered traditions of the middle ages and reverted to the Vedas in their original form for solution to the problem. In Bengal, Sarat Chandra Chatterjee showed many aspects of women in contemporary rural and urban Bengal. In **Shubhada** (1898) he shows the widow Lalana pursued by perverse fate and callous society, finally, finding her answer in refusing remarriage (but not love). **Chota Bhai** (1912) shows the evil a cruel hearted widow can do by trying to dominate over others. **Arakshaniya** shows how a widow has to face the bitter tongues of the in-laws. These examples, to name but a few and random ones, may show how the domestic novel developed in Indian literatures and gave varied and powerful characters of Indian women. The woman had come to be the centre of fiction in Bengali and Marathi literatures.

In the Indo-Anglian novels of this time a slow but sure change is seen. The titles themselves speak of the writers' increasing preoccupation with the problems of women. After Bankim's novel **Raj Mohan's Wife** (1864) there was a lull followed by novels by other writers. **Kamala, a Story of Hindu Wife** (1894) and **Saguna, a Study of Native Christian Life** (1895) are by Krupabai Sathianandhan, and **The Hindu Wife** (1876) by Raj Laxmi Devi, **Batoabai A Sketch of a Bombay High Caste Hindu Young Wife** (1890) by Shevantabai Nikambe are all by women novelists. Many can be seen showing their interest in women-**Sarala and Hingana** (1895) by Khetrapal Chakrawarti, **Love of Kusuma** (1911) by J.J. Singh. Though mostly forgotten now, these novels are significant as illustrating the trend in bringing the women to the fore in the novel. Indo-Anglian as well as Indian novels reveal struggle to coordinate the divergent cultures of the East and West in the image of the women. Generally, she is shown as the heroine of the novel. At times, she combines what is regarded as best of both the worlds. She is educated, charming, an object of romantic love. **Indulekha** (n.d.) a Malyalam novel, shows the heroine well versed in English as well as in Sanskrit. The writer, fully aware that there are no such women in reality, almost apologetically explains in his preface that he created this women as an ideal heroine. **Indulekha** replaces the romantic heroine of Sanskrit fiction by the romantic heroine borrowed from English fiction, or rather mixes up both to form a single image. This romantic image of the heroine with mixed East-West ideals later became a staple of Indo-Anglian fiction as well as of fiction in most Indian language.

Most often, novelists portray two heroines in the novel, symbolizing the Indian and the Western conceptions. The Indian girl is sweet, charming, capable of deep and silent love and sacrifice. The other girl is educated, with Western values and in Bengali fiction she generally hails from Brahmo

Samaj and from the city. In Tagor's **Wreck** (1919) Kamala stands for the Indian values of silent suffering, deep faithful love and hard-work. At the other end, is Hemnalini, an educated girl coming from the Brahmo Samaj, yet equally charming, though paler in comparison . the fact that though Kamala is put to the test of fate's perversity to a great length, and is yet rewarded in the end, shows the tilt in the direction of extolling the Indian value, though a direct collision is skilfully avoided by Tagore. But many novelsshow the Indian girl pitted against the West-educated girl. The Indian girl generally wins (at times only in the spiritual sense of suffering) in the end. The mother does not figure much in Anglo-Indian fiction but she appears often in Indian as well as in Indo-Anglian fiction. In Tagore's **Gora** (1923) Anandamoyi's mother-love transcends caste and race when she adopts a white orphan. In **Wreck**, Kshemnkari is pure, holy, kind, loving, sacrificing, the centre of the home. Like the epic mothers they are venerable, and reflect clearly the ancient Indian culture. As to the reality about the influence of the mother on the children, Nirad Choudhari's remarks are helpful. He observes about his own mother; 'her face did not show, hardly indicated even, the immense sense of her moral convictions', and admiringly refers to 'my mother's honesty'.(Chaudhri,1971,165) Though he differed from her in other intellectual matters, the moral influence of his mother shaped his character. In many a novel the mother's influence on her children will be seen shaping, guiding and protecting them.

No doubt, the very early Indian writers had not cared much to produce realistic or naturalistic fiction. They wrote romances, and when they turned to write novels with social themes, there was a heavy mixture of Western romance, sentimentality or idealism. But with Sarat Chandra in Bengali and Prem Chand in Hindi the trend of realism spread. Prem Chand's **Sevasadan** (1916) showed the reality of the Indian prostitute, while Sarat Chandra showed women in rural and urban circles from the middle or lower middle class. The same movement towards realism shows up in Indo-Anglian fiction, with Mulk Raj Anand, who turned his attention to the lowest of the low. His **Untouchable** became an immediate success.

In fact Kamala Merkandaya's opereative life, from **Nectar in a Seieve** (1954) to **Pleasure City**(1984) spans the three eventful decades in the history of Indian women. The beginning of the process or emancipation of Indian women that E. M. Forster hints at in his fascinating essay "*India Again*" was greatly accelerated in the decades following India's Independence. E. M. Forster writes, "No-externally India has not changed. And this changelessness in her is called by some observers 'the real India'. I don't myself like the phrase 'the real India'. I suspect it. It always makes me prick up my ears. But you can use it if you want to, either for the changes in her or for the unchanged. 'Real is at the service of all schools of the thought, it is when you leave the country, or the streets of the town, and go into the private houses, that you begin to notice a second great alteration, second only to politics—namely the lifting of purdah, the increasing emancipation of women. It struck me particularly in cities which are largely Moslem, such as Lahore and Hyderabad, where women once kept rigidly behind the veil. I have been in my life three times to Hyderabad, some of my happiest Indian days were spent there, so I have been able to trace this change. My first visit was in 1912 and then I saw scarcely any Indian women. My second visit was in 1921 when I was admitted into some family circles and saw a good deal of what may be called 'semi-purdah'- ladies coming out into company, but not coming avowedly, and retiring at any moment behind the vail if they felt disposed except amongst the most conservative, and at the receptions to which I went the women sometimes out-numbered the men. Since they kept to their lovely Indian saris, the effect was exquisite; it was a delight to look round at so much gracefulness and graciousness, at so many and such well-chosen colours. I don't know how far into society this lifting of the vail has extended. But I imagine that sooner or later the change will extend to the villages and transform the

Indian social fabric from top to bottom. Our world does not go back, though whether it progresses God alone knows, and in India, as in the west, women will shortly have the same opportunities as men for good and for evil." (Krishnamurti, 1966, 112-3)

Nevertheless, the induction of women in Indian Administrative and Foreign Services, in management and entrepreneurship, Bar, judiciary, education, medical profession; if their elevation to the Prime Ministership of India is any token of the transformation of the "Indian social fabric", then there has been definite progress in this important sphere of our national life. Significantly this tremendous breakthrough after years of privacy and purdah coincides with as most fertile period of Kamala Markandaya creative life. While she wrote her novels about women caught in the drama of ravage and ruin the man-woman scenario registered dramatic changes in India. To take a few concrete examples, Smt Vijay Lakshmi Pandit presided over the U.N. General Assembly, Smt. Indira Gandhi rose to become a powerful Prime Minister, Arati Saha the first Indian woman swimmer, crossed the English channel, and Bachendri Paul planted the Indian tricolour top the Mt Everest. These are tokens of great changes in different walks of Indian life with women coming in increasingly larger numbers to occupy important positions in police, banking and other services. Many of them have become members of the State Assemblies and the national Parliament.

In the novels of Kamala Markandaya these women should have registered this important process of change of her fiction. The struggle for independence and Mahatma Gandhi's contribution to it find a fairly large representation in Indo-Anglian fiction. Anand has written with feeling and urgency about the untouchables, coolies and labourers in the tea-gardens. How is it that the woman have received scant attention even from the women writers? Perhaps in a vast country like India the above mentioned examples are only of statistical value as these constitute only the tip of the iceberg. The sun-lit tip can hardly obscure the larger reality of the huge black mass suspended underneath. Kamla Markandaya paints her woman characters as suppressed, burdened and suffering creatures whose redeeming qualities are faith and the capacity to burn stoically in the crucible of suffering. Kamala Markandaya's Rukmani, Mira, Srojini and Lalitha represent facets of this woman figure who is at the back of the author's mind. This Sita-Savitri type or stereotype dominates the consciousness of Mrs. Markandaya. She is a novelist who creates her stories by weaving together the images and impressions floating in her mind. Perhaps the above mentioned changes make no difference to Kamala Markandaya's world as the great earthquakes of history such as Napoleonic wars made no impact on Jane Austen's fiction. The women characters of Kamala Markandaya are embodiments of the conception of Indian women stored in her subconscious mind. We look for the reflection of real-life models or real-life situations in fiction due to a lack of proper under-standing of the creative process. It is too often forgotten that a literary work is not a picture taken by a photographic camera and that to the degree that the artist is creative, what he has taken from experience is thrown into the furnace of mind, where often, at depths far beyond the reach of consciousness it loses its identity and gains, new form, new significance, and a capacity for resonance that is altogether lacking before the act of composition.

Such women forged in the smithy of Kamala Markandaya's mind give no evidence of a deep understanding of their various manifestations the women seem to be suffering, if not defeated creatures. Rukmani for all her suffering draws "nectar in a sieve", and Sarojini clings to the life of faith symbolized by Swamiji. Mira is described by some critics as "Mother India" because torn between personal love for Richard and the impersonal love for her motherland, she shows determination between sobs-the determination to support the patriotic cause. There are other female characters who fit into the expected pattern. Nalini of **A Handful of Rice** sticks to Ravi braving the onslaughts of misfortune. Granny and Aunt Alemelu are old women symbolizing the ancient way. They resist change, and are suspicious of everything that smacks of modernity. In **Two Virgins** the equations are too simplistic to permit deeper understanding of character or situation. Aunt Almelu has a premonition of misfortune hovering over Lalitha because her fascination for the city culture. She hates Mr Gupta, the film producer and Miss Mendoza, the Principal of the Convent School, "She disapproved of Miss Mendoza's ways which were modern".(Markandaya,1977,57) If we add to this Caroline' and Helen we have a nearly complete view of Markandaya's stereo\types. Caroline being a western woman is a temptress. She represents national values and the life of sensuality. Perhaps in the clash of cultures in Markandaya presents her as the very antithesis of Nalini, the sacrificing Indian woman. A western woman is invariably painted as a creature wanting in something essential without which no happiness is possible, and for this they come to India or are drawn to the sadhus and swamis.

The prejudices and taboos surrounding Indian women are shown by Kamala Markandaya, by Kunthi in **A Nectar in a Sieve,** a bad woman because she lives by extortion and prostitution. But Ira in the same novel draws our sympathy even though she too lives by prostitution. She plays the role of the life-sustainer, because with the earnings she sustains her brothers and sisters. The Indian woman is a victim of many prejudices and she has to meet the endless expectations of a male-dominated ancient society. Ira is cast away by her husband because she is barren, and Aunt Almelu is a woman without any right, social or human, because she is a widow. Virginity is yet another factor on which hinges the prospect of conjugal love. Discovering blood on their marriage bad Ravi is overwhelmed with joy: "It induced in him a protective flood of tenderness for Nalini". (Markandaya,1966,64) Nothing really changes in the world of Kamala Markandaya with the changing times. Somehow the old ways and attitudes persist and women continue to stagger under the heavy yoke of an ancient society not quite amenable to change. Let us consider the attitudes as they crystallize in the following conversation between the representatives of the ancient and modern ways in **Two Virgins**:

Appa cleared his throat. He said young women these days did go in for careers and he brought out that, yes, his daughter might have one too. What had she in mind? He asked Miss Mendoza, and nothing was more clear than that his was quite blank.

> Teaching said Miss Mendoza, which turned Amma to stone, some kind of glittering rock which you felt would draw blood if you so much as touched it. So no one attempted to move except Miss Mendoza who was courageous who said bravely that in England, where she had done her training, it was a respectable occupation, but Amma said NOT for any daughter of mine, in tones that would have shriveled up anyone. (Markandaya,1977,234)

By the end of the novel the forebodings of Amma comes true. The path to hell is paved with the myriad attractions of modern life. At the end, Lalitha, the darling of Miss Mndoza finds herself in hell. To Saroja Amma says: Your sister wandered too far, she said wearily, she was lured outside the code of our community and is paying that penalty, that is all. (Markandaya, 1977,239) Women, modern or ancient, are destined to suffer in the world of Kamala Markandaya. Suffering is the common lot of Rukmani, the peasant woman, Mira, the educated woman, and Lalitha, the young girl lured by the city culture. In extolling suffering, passive endurance and making her women adapt themselves to the humour and pleasure of their male partners, Kamala Markanaya is merely recreating the Sita-Savitri types. Perhaps these types come to the surface like bubbles from the depth of her subconscious mind, or perhaps, Kamala Markandaya is conscious of the dominance of the ancient ways beneath the veneer of modernity. After all in this ancient land the past and present have a simultaneous presence. Even as women march ahead scaling the Mount Everest and entering field of life with resolute steps, they burn as Sati or are burnt for dowry. Whatever the attitude of Kamala Markandaya towards women in "real" life she is to be judged on the basis of the creative presentation of women in her fiction. It seems that Kamala Markandaya could not look beyond the stereotypes that came easily to her mind. In interpreting the strength of women as creatures of faith she failed to make a distinction between faith and blind faith. And in not being able to explore the fascinating subject of the place of woman in a joint family system she wasted a great opportunity. What Kamala Markandaya gives us is a contrived picture wanting in depth and authenticity. It is better to conclude with the observations of M.K. Naik,

"Kamala Markandaya's picture of rustic life in **Nectar in a Seive** (1954) and **Two Virgins** (1973) are as superficial as her attempt at low class urban realism in **A Handful of Rice** (1966) is unconvincing. There is far greater authenticity in stray chronicles of social life in Hindu, Muslim and Parsi households by less known women novelists, who mostly wrote little more than a novel each: Venu Chitale's **In Transit** (1959) - a story of three generations of a Poona Brahmin joint family between the two world wars; Ram Mehta's **Inside the Haveli** (1917) - an absorbing account of Rajasthani purdah life; two studies of Muslim life; Zeenuth Futhally's **Zohra** (1951) with the princely state of Hyderabed in the Gandhian age as its setting, and Attia Hosain's **Sunlight On a Broken Coumn** (1961), a nostalgic account of aristocratic life in pre-partition Lucknow; and Perin Bhrucha's vivid presentation of Parsi Life in **Fire Worshippers** (1968). Equally interesting are ethnological studies by men, including B.K. Karanjia's novel of Parsi life in Bombay: **More of an Indian** (1970) and Leslie de Noronha's account of colonial Goan life: **The Mango and the Tamarind Tree** (1970). (Naik,1984,109-10)

This is what Kamala is and for what she stands and writes.

REFERENCES

1. *Poets and Story Tellers*, Constable, London, 1960, p. 100.
2. Forster, E.M., *Virginia Woolf*, ed., Claire Sprague, New Delhi, Prentice-Hall, 1971.
3. Markandaya, Kamala, *A Silence of Desire*, Four Square Books, London, 1966.
4. Markandaya, Kamala, A *Handful of Rice*, Orient Paperbacks, New Delhi, 1966.
5. Markandaya, Kamala, *Two Virgins*, Vikas Publishing House, New Delhi, 1977.
6. Markandaya, Kamala, *Some Inner Fury*, Putnam & Co., London, 1955.
7. Markandaya, Kamala, *The Nowhere Man*,Orient Longman, Bombay, 1975.
8. Joseph, Margaret P., *Kamala Markandaya*, Arnold Heinemann New Delhi, 1980.
9. Kurtz, Paul, *The Fullness of Life*, Horizon Press, New York, 1974.
10. Markandaya, Kamala, *Pleasure City*, Chatto and Windus, London, 1982.
11. Gokak, V.K., "English in India" - All India Teachers Conference, 11th Session, Delhi, 1960, Presidential Address, pp. 52-53.
12. K.R.S. Iyengar, The Study of Indian Writing in Engiish Lectures at Leeds Uiversity, 1959 (Popular, Bombay, 1959) p. 4.
13. Mukherjee, Meenakshi, *The Twice Born Fiction*, New Delhi, London, Heinemann, 1972.
14. Quoted in C. Paul Verghese, *Problems of the Indian Creative Writer in English*, Bombay, Somaiya Publications, 1971.
15. Frazer, R.W., Literary History of India (1898), London, Fisher Unwin, 1920.
16. Iyengar, K.R.S, *Indian Writing in English*, Bombay, Asia Publishing House, 2nd Ed., 1973.
17. Dutt, Romesh Chander, *The Lake of Palma*, McMillan, 1933.

18. Chaudhari, Nired C., *The Autobiography of an unknown Indian* Londdon, McMillan & Co. Ltd., Jaico Impresion, 1971.

19. Krishnamurti, R., ed., *E.M. Forster*, "India Again: Selections from E.M. Forster, The McMillan Company of India Ltd, 1966.

20. Naik, M., *Dimensions of Indian English Literature,* Sterling Publishers, Bombay, 1984.

3

The 'Other' in Kamala and Others

Normally, a woman in an Indian family, as portrayed in the Indo-Anglian novels, is more a traditional image than a rebellious one. Traditionally, she is accepted in the framework of the family with a blind faith and rarely showed a rebellious trend. She continued to be docile, self-sacrificing, patient, loving and capable of suffering. Later, when she moved into society, she became bolder and more individualistic. Most women shown in the Indo-Anglian fiction belong to the first category. They suffer, submit and adjust themselves to circumstances. This aspect of woman's life has been portrayed by the women writers with sensitivity and instinctive understanding.Women who are rebels, who reject the established norms and come out of the family set-up are found initially in the novels dealing with the freedom movement or in the novels projecting the East-West conflict. The efforts of reformers such as Raja Ram Mohan Roy, Mahatma Phule. Agarkar and others initiated a change in the situation. However, it was Gandhi's call to women that had a stirring effect. The old and the young, the bold and the timid, the rich and the poor joined to the non-violent struggle led by Gandhi. Their whole-hearted participation in the struggle for emancipation indicated that they had acquired enough moral courage.

We have novels like **Kandan, The Patriot, Inquilab,** where women appear in the freedom struggle but are drawn in a sketchy way. However, the whole saga of the struggle of women in the Gandhian period is shown vividly in Raja Rao's **Kanthapura** (1938). No other novel has shown at once so delicately and so broadly a picture of what happened to the women in hundreds of villages in India. We have here a vivid picture of women living in their village-world unchanged from ancient times, waking at last to a barb knowledge, transmuting it into their personal experiences. These women shed their age-old taboos of caste, educate themselves, give speeches, and face lathi-charges. For them, it is a great leap from the past to the present. Awakening comes to these women through religious stories. They hear the Harikathaman telling them that Earth, Brahama's daughter, is enslaved by men coming from beyond the seas, that Mohandas goes from village to village to slay the serpent of foreign rule. Rangama tells them of

> "The universe floating in the diamond-dust of God.... That gave us a shiver, I tell you, that we would not sit alone in the kitchen that night or the night after". (Rao, 1947, 52)

The sudden widening of the horizons of knowledge makes the women dizzy and forces them out of the kitchens which had been their place from times immoral. Gradually, the effect of education makes the women challenge age-old taboos. They hear from Rangama of a land, ten times as big as Mysore, where women work like men, night and day, and get three months' holiday when it is born. They know then, by comparison, perhaps for the first time, their sad plight caused by slavery and orthodoxy. Ratna, a child-widow, is sent to school. She

> "not only went about the streets like a boy, but even wore her hair to the left like a concubine and she still kept her bangles and her nose-ring and ear-rings and when she was asked why she behaved as though

> she had not lost her husband, she said that, that was nobody's business, and that if these sniffing old country hens thought that seeing a man for a day, and this when one is ten years of age, could be called a marriage, they had better eat mud and drown themselves in the river".(Rao,1947,42)

This impudent assertion provokes her own mother Kamalamma to say that she should never have been sent to school. For Ratna, the young widow, it was perhaps natural to rebel. Not so for the older women whose minds were moulded by the old traditions. The hardest taboo was of caste, and Moorthy's own mother died out of sorrow when she heard that her son had started mixing with the pariahs. The scales of ignorance fall slowly from the eyes of these women lying in the torpor of ages. Their joining the spinning movement is their first active step in the freedom struggle. Until then it was only a passive role - that of listening to the Harikethaman or to Rangamama. Even then very few are inspired by a purely patriotic motive. Many need some feminine enticement. So Moorthy tells one if she will have bodice-cloth, another that she will have a peacock-coloured same for a marriage in the house, a third needy housewife a bit of money to lay by religion, knowledge, a bit of personal enticement, all join together in bringing these women to a national awareness. Then they all feel they must form a 'Sevika Sangha' and they call themselves sevis. But as these women cross the threshold to step into the freedom struggle, they carry their feminine nature with them. When they decide to welcome Moorthy some say the will wear their Dharamwar saree and diamond hair flower, others their gold-belts. Widows will wear only the gold-belt and necklace, now that they cannot wear bangles. Ratna thinks she will part her hair to the left, apply a tiny kumkum mark and wear her saree to reach her toes. Thus, though they are sevis, they are very selective about their dress. In the words of C.D.Narasimhaiah "the novelist's irony cuts both ways". (Narsimhiah, 1968, 217) When the women actually form their Sevi-Sanghs, to out and start learning how to be disciplined and courageous, their men folk become jealous and suspicious. So when the milk curdles or a dhoti is not dry, it is attributed to the Sevi business. But the tactful Rangamma works out compromises which pacify husbands and leave the women free to work for the movement.

We find the obstacle of male objection removed, but the women find it difficult to overcome their own feeling of fear. Rangamma finds she can only stutter a few words and is choked with tears when she tries to give a speech. When the women start their lessons in courage and non-violence, how to face the police-lathis calmly, it proves an ordeal. Here again the domestic and the social spheres overlap. A woman dreams that her husband beats her, not with hands, but with a stick, and he was Bade Khan. But the urge to participate in the Mahatma's movement does not let them rest. There is a gradual mental readiness, an anticipation of the struggle they will have to undergo. These women, who had hardly stopped beyond the threshold, are ready to march behind Moorthy, and the image of Mahatma rises like the Sahyadri Mountains to cheer them. If a woman loses courage, cries or trembles, another consoles her in familiar words which both understand. They remain together during the toddy-picketing and face police atrocities. It is a revelation to the women that they can help and save one another if they are united. This experience brings women to a sense of oneness with the poor, and their shyness and fears are gone. There is a new awareness of the knowledge others have gained, a desire to gain freedom, because they know that they are one and they know'our men were not far and their eye did not shut'. (Rao,1947,217) With this assurance they face bullets in a field Satyagraha. They lose their houses but this experience of coming out of their age-old restrictions and participating in the mass-movement fills their hearts with abundance like the Gauri Lights on the Himavaty. There is loss on the material plane but they are enriched in their souls. These women have come out of the stagnant pools of orthodoxy and have merged in the national current.

However, the novelist has, realistically shown some dark corners which remain unrelieved by either the freedom struggle or by education. The women in the coffee estate fall victims to the Red man's lust and slave for two-anna bits. Virago Venkamma is still strident. Concubine Chinna still lures customers. But the women who have participated in the freedom movement have their hearts enriched, their minds broadened, and they feel a sense of fulfillment. Though there is loss on the material and individual plane, their houses and fields gone, they experience a deep satisfaction and serenity of mind. Even the old grand-mother from the most orthodox section - the Brahmin middle-class in the village experience it. She does not mind the loss of her house Rangamma and Ratna have both led the women and they have felt a new awakening in their lives.

No doubt, Raja Rao has shown a grandmother as an active participant in the movement. An orthodox creature, she becomes a participant and a promoter of the freedom movement. The grandmother in **A Goddess Named Gold** (1980) by Bhabani Bhattacharya, who too is shown with great insight, helps to bring about the emanicipation of the village women in a similar way. Though she suffers from gout, she participates in the processions against the Seth. Her very presence gives courage to the timid village women and frightens the Seth. **The Chicago Tribune** critic calls her the book's most remarkable character.

Aa we know, Indo-Anglian fiction is that very few novels depict participation of women in society and the freedom movement which brought about a great change in their lives. There is no portrayal of women in prison. This shows the inability of the Indo-Anglian writers to grapple with full reality of emancipated womanhood in India. It seems that most of the writers themselves (women writers specially) were not active participants in this great movement. The superficiality in the depiction of women in the movement by women writers is due to their lack of understanding the great phenomenon. One catches just a few glimpses of the freedom movement **In Transit** by Venu Chitale. **Zohra** (1951) by Zeenuth Fathehally shows the unfulfilled love. **Sunlight on a Broken Column** (1961) by Attia Husain shows the heroine Leila looking through the chinks of her purdah-closed world at lathi charged processions and her wounded cousins. Mira, the narrator-heroine of **Some Inner Fury** (1955) by Kamala Markandaya, comes to know of the terrorist movement through her cousins and of the Gandhian movement through Roshan. The latter is happy in a gay as well as a Khaddar dress, just as she moves with ease among fashionable people and freedom fighters. She is a rare example of a woman who courts arrest and enters prison. But her life in the prison is not shown.

These characters, lacking authentic touch, the images given by some men writers of women participating in the freedom struggle are bolder and more powerful in spite of the fact that their main preoccupation is with the hero. Bharati, in R.K. Narayan's **Waiting for the Mahatma** (1955) appears before Sriram's vision as a sparkling and happy creature. She fascinates him and he is drawn to Gandhi's ashram. Though an orphan in the ashram, she is high-spirited and ripples with laughter like a clear mountain stream. All the duties of the ashram like spinning, helping the downtrodden, are done by her with ease. She even joins the Satyagraha, courts arrest and enters prison. To her, Gandhi is father and she follows his orders, in prison or out of it. She moves with ease in the ashram and among all the people crowding around Gandhi. She even looks after the orphans of the partition. Nirmala in **Chronicles of Kedaram** (1961) by Nagarajan is a motherless but talented girl married to a moron and separated. She too turns to the poor and the harijans and tries to reclaim the workers from the toddy shops. But she enters the novel rather late and her life in the asram is not shown to us. Further, she does not appear to have inspired or activated people around her. She is, rather, a victim of suspicions, scandals and doubts. She may be taken as a representation of those women who tuned to the Gandhian ashram as a home, as a place of safety, from this world of sorrows.

We find that the Gandhian principles of asceticism led women to suppress or spirititualize their personal desires. Suruchi, the wife of Satyajit in Bhattacharya's **Shadow from Ladakh** was educated at Shantiniketan. She and Satyajit had met and married in Shantiniketan and had shared aesthetic values. Life was a sweet music for Suruchi. Then Saatyajit came under the Gandhian influence and adopted asceticism. Suruchi found, to her dismay, that he started avoiding her at home. If he came to her drawn by a sexual urge, he felt ashamed and guilty. She felt she had lost her womanly dignity by this attitude of her husband. She was for life, happiness, beauty, motherhood. She had aesthetic sense inherent in her and heightened by Tagore's Shantiniketan. But Satyajit's asceticism was anti-life as his friend Biresh had pointed out. He put his ideals to test at the cost of his wife's happiness. She had to suppress her for a son and all her womanly urges, and finally she had to allow her own daughter to be brought up in Satyajit's pattern. As mother it pained her to see that Sunita wore no bangles, dressed like a widow and followed Satyajit's asceticism. She felt a hidden sympathy for Jhanak, the untouchable girl, who was alive and full of desires. When Satyajit sent her to Russia, her horizons widened and Suruchi who returned home was a different women. Now she could look beyond her home, her ashram, and see the Chinese and the Russian women, and observe how bold and asserting they were. The face had a new touch of brightness now. After her first speech the ashramites commented "Always she has been our happiness and now she is our great pride". (Bhattacharya, 1967, 63)

On the other hand, Suruchi had grown to her full stature, her abilities weie seen by all. Like Kasturba she had to be not only a "spiritual companion"(Bhattacharya,1967,65) to her husband but she had to perform social duties in the ashram as well. During her trip to Moscow, "she had discovered unknown sources of power in herself". Bhattacharya,1967,101) But as her social sphere widened, there arose, as her daughter perceived, "some new discontent". (Bhattacharya,1967,102)Satyajit thought she had 'perfectly adapted to the mould he had set' but he did know that she was 'in the grip of an unaccustomed revolt'. (Bhattacharya,1967,106) She was coming out of the shadow of the Kasturba image to take her place in society. But to this realistic struggle and emergence of woman the novelist gives a romantic ending.

And Sumita, her daughter, wore white and went without the kumkum mark and bangles. Though the women in the ashram did not like young girls to be dressed like widows, she followed her father's ascetic ideals and wore white. She was totally ignorant of the desires of the body having more of the spiritual element in her and this drew her away from Jhanak who was given to desires. She was like the spinning wheel, symbolizing Gandhian vales, while Rupa, the Eurasian girl, was, as Bhaskar puts it, like the turbine. But Sumita was brought up in the small world of the ashram and she too, like Suruchi, underwent the experience of going out in a wider world to see for herself other values which were also noble. Thus she had a chance to compare what she saw with her ashramite life. Teaching children, spinning, living a pure life were the things she did before she went to Delhi. There she saw girls and women helping at the stalls put up to cheer soldiers going to the front. All this was so new to her that she had to evaluate her former ideals over again. It was this wider knowledge that enabled her to work for a harmonious compromise between Steel Town and Gandhigram, the new and old forces, duty and love. In the old, both the women not only come out of the Gandhian or rather the ascetic principles of Satyajit but go beyond it to blend the ascetic and the aesthetic (Gandhi and Tagore) ways of life, or Gandhigram and Steel Town (Gandhi and Nehru), the spinning wheel and the turbine (East and West). Women in this novel serve to bring about social harmony. The Gandhian principles carried to the extreme by Satyajit are detrimental to life. So they blend them with reality to make a better society and in the process, create happiness for themselves and for others.

While the early Indo-Anglian novels had shown woman in the family, the novels after 1940 begin to reflect woman participating in the freedom struggle, imbibing knowledge, experiencing a sense of emancipation. However, such novels are few. Woman novelists are more engrossed in portraying the palpitating hearts of the heroines and show only glimpse of the woman's role in the freedom movement. Their social work is just to drown their disappointment. The life of the Satyajit women is not touched at all. Though woman was struggling to come out of the state of stagnation, women-writers have neglected this aspect.

The middle class women were rarely permitted to leave their homes even for a job, till the forties. This may be one reason why only the lower class earning woman is found in the early Indo-Anglian fiction appears to have come out of her home into society but as a matter of fat she carries the silent suffering attitude to her place of work. The image of the working woman becomes an extension of the silent suffering pativarata Stri, (the devoted, suffering wife). At home she is beaten by her husband and the spirit of revolt is crushed out of her. Her image, as a worker, is that of a mule-like worker.

We find that in the thirties, writers seem to have noticed this downtrodden, suffering, lower class woman worker. Mulk Raj Anand shows women working, suffering and submitting silently to the conditions around them. Laxmi in **Coolie** (1936) works meekly, almost cheerfully, in adverse conditions. The thought of rebellion never enters her mind. Sajani and Laila in **Two Leaves and a Bud** (1937) also work submissively and silently at home and on the plantation, as do nearly all the rest of the women workers. The women collies in **Kanthapura** (1933) work silently, submissively till the police atrocities ravage their plantation. Yet, we see all these characters from the outside. What Laxmi in **Coolie** felt, what Sohini in **Untouchable** suffered, what the coolie-women in **Kanthapura** went through is not fully articulated. Had these working women from the lower classes been shown in all their inner experience, there would have been a completely different and sensitive picture of the lower class working women in Indo-Anglian novels. The difference such a treatment makes may be seen in the image of Kajoli, a creature of joy and love in So **Many Hungers** (1947) by Bhabani Bhattacharya, Kajoli works on the farm at first, but a harsh famine crushes her from all sides. Yet she saves her spirit by helping others and by distributing bread the destitute.

We find that the rebellion that rises in a woman's heart against working conditions is many a time smothered by the authority of the male in the family or by the pressure of circumstances. This is found in Rukmani, a straight-forward and hard-working peasant woman of **Nectar in a Sieve** (1954) by Kamala Markandaya. Rukmani works hard and she is proud of the way of her life. She is at first happy and satisfied to work in the peaceful South-Indian village. But the starting of the tannery disturbs the rhythm of her life and she is unhappy to see her sons drawn to the tannery, but her voice is of no avail for it is the father who takes the decision. Later, natural calamity like flood and famine drive them out of their home and all her rebellion is crushed into sorrow, though she remains beside her husband in all the dull painful period of her stone-cutting work in the city. It is her stoical way of facing calamities that itself impresses on our minds. She is the only working woman in the entire novel who has rebellious thoughts which she was forced to suppress. Her rebellion is not against natural calamities but against man-made conditions. She faces the flooded field with a stoic sorrow but she is upset by the evil pollution caused by the tannery, by the purdah-clad women and by the immoral city-men. However, in spite of her being spiritedly vocal on several matters at the beginning, she frequently surrenders to the male-dominated traditions. She has sympathy for the husband who casts away his wife because she bears no children. In spite of her strong disapproval of her children working in the tannery, she accepts meekly with her husband decides about them because the man is the head of the Hindu family, the father is authorized to decide about the children. Her views about Kenny, the missionary, however, are her own. She even tells her son not to think of what people say and allows him to work with Kenny. But the death of her sons so numbs her brain that she has no strength left to say anything to the tannery officials or to the agent who evicts them. Poverty crushes out the spirit in Rukmani. The change in the status and spirit of woman after the beginning of the 20th century has been noted by sociologists.

> In the last fifty years or so, India has witnessed profound changes in almost every aspect of her life. Since the advent of independence in August, 1947, the pace of change has greatly accelerated. (Kapur, 1972, 3)

As Dr. Promila Kapur finds the change has led to "the emancipation of women from the tradition-bound ethos - the newly emerging middle-class working woman in India".... These women experiencing "a socio-economic emanicipation".(Kapur,1972,13) In her pioneer work in this field she finds that the conditions in the West do not apply to Indian situations where, as in a joint family, there was greater companionship and a prescribed formula for one's rights and duties. The reason for the woman's submissive role, as Dr. Radhakrishnan points out, is that "centuries of traditions have made the Indian women the most patient women in the world, whose pride is suffering". (Kapur, 1972, 10)

In such a changed situation woman, too, is changing. She is experiencing a conflict of values. She does not feel confident of her ability to combine the two roles of woman, the woman in the family and the woman as a worker, without disturbing the harmony of family life. As more and more middle-class women try to get jobs this becomes more and more serious. The middle-class working woman, a product of education and economic conditions, appears in the novels after the forties. More recent Indo-Anglian novels tell us more about the motivations and reactions of women who work. Mulk Raj Anand, who writes mostly about the lower classes, shows in **The Old Woman and the Cow** (1960), a docile girl from the peasant class, revolting against a malignant mother-in-law and a mother-dominated husband. The road she has to tread to the city for self-reliance is a hard one, but she does not flinch.

As we see, the first half of the twentieth century did not receive the middle-class women very warmly when they tried to be working women. The opposition (overt and covert) at home, the suspicion and the scorn of society, the moral predicament in their own divided minds caused tensions for them in their efforts to stand on their own leg. This material offered a good opportunity to the creative imagination for vivid and touching portrayal of the dilemma and the despair, of the suffering and the frustration of the middle-class working women, however, the opportunity was lost and what actually resulted was a superficial treatment of their life. The women received attention more for their romantic conflicts with men than for themselves. It is also surprising that most of the working women shown in Indo-Anglian fiction belong to the Christian community even through instances of Hindu and Muslim working women are not frequent. Perhaps the writers thought the Eurasian or the Christian woman more amenable to the romantic set up of the novel. Mohini (**Music for Mohini**) or Sumita and Suruchi (**Shadow from Ladakh**) teach children because they like to do so. But Rupa, a Eurasian secretary, in the latter novel teaches the Chinese children because she is enamoured of the engineer of Steel Town and this gives her an opportunity to visit him. She herself comes from a broken home, has a past and she tries to lure the engineer to herself. She does not appear to be dissatisfied with her working conditions. Even Suruchi is shown to be happy with the children in the ashram-school, but the conflict of aesthetic and ascetic ways of life which is clearly worked out in her home-life is not shown in her work, though the ashram itself is ultimately preaching a philosophy of life which she disapprove at home.

Though in general the experience of women in their working conditions has not been fully explored by the creative writers, there are some happy exceptions where a woman's life at work is as convincingly portrayed as her life at home. As a working woman, or instance, the Secretary Mrs.Mehra in **Shadow from Ladakh** is unique. She is a convincing image. Though she is plump, she rides a bike. Her husband addresses her as Mrs. Sarojini Mehra and they indulge in the mild teasing of each other. But they have a deep regard for each other. When she advertises for a bride for the C.K., she goes all the way on her bicycle to let out the secret to her husband, only to him, though her ability to keep secrets is great.

> The files in Room Nineteen have so many top secrets. Not one of them will ever pass my lips, not even if I am tortured, hacked up limb my limb, But this...this...is too much for a woman to endure. (Bhattachrya, 1967, 97)

Her efficiency is admirable. She faces the women at the Club, at Meadow House; she persuades Bhaskar the C.E. to be the caretaker of the Chinese children. When she senses a crisis due to Rupa's stay, she persuades her to leave. She is the image of a very efficient secretary, though she has a mind of her own. The touch of humour and the bit of crudeness in her home-life save her from being too much of an idealized image. Mrs. Mehra conforms to the pervasive mother-image in Indian life, while Rupa is the sexy Anglo-Indian involved in the romantic affairs of men.Though women in various fields of work are found in Malgonkar's novels too, they are not always convincing. Ruby Mirenda is headmistress of an estate school in **Combat of Shadows** (1962). She is there, not really as headmistress, but for other reasons, as Henry Winton finds:

> The rare mixture of the submissiveness and surrender of oriental womanhood with the freedom and gaiety of the West, and of course the breathtaking figure

> and good looks and colouring which had been a gift of both the West and the East. (Malgonker, 1963, 112)

Her post as Headmistress is just a convenience. She is not shown in her work and so she does not appear convincing in it. These women exist for the men, if at all they can be said to exist. Dr. Amur's comment is significant.Malgonkar's women characters have never been fully credible.(Amur,1973,65) Ruby does not come to life in her environment as Mrs. Mehra, Rupa, Sumita or Suruchi. Even Minnie Bradley of **The Princes** (1963), 'an Anglo-Indian girl who had to work for a living'.(Malgonker,1963,151) She enters Abhay's life and only part of her life that is known to Abhay is revealed. The working women is not taken seriously by Malgonkar. There hovers as if or rootless decadence about the working Anglo-Indian women in his novels. They appear exotic, unconvincing.

Unpredictably, the middle-class working woman is not shown convincingly even in the novels by women writers. The writer-reporter is just a sensitive and sympathetic reflector in **Possession** (1963) by Kamala Markandaya. Her visits to Madras or London and her writing is obviously a excuse for her to be near Val. She broods on his future but her reactions to her own work remain unknown to us. Mira and Roshan in **Some Inner Fury** (1955-57) work in a press. Mira's mildly rebellious reactions are shown. The lead is apparently given by Roshan who is bold, free and confident. She takes Mira to the press and guides her. Mira in this world is a struggling, sensitive creature who wants work, less for money than for driving out boredom, the gadfly of the rich. The reader gets a few glimpse of the working environment but is soon whisked away with Mira who is sent to gather reports of an English sponsored project which lands her in Richard's office. Obviously, her work is only a ruse to introduce her in the land of romance. As more and more middle-class women entered jobs, sociologists and writers were bond to reflect their problems and the former casual attitude gave place to more attentive undertakings. The rise of the working woman in middle-class has led to pioneer sociological surveys by Dr. Promilla Kapur and other sociologists. In case study 193, Mrs. G's individual satisfaction in work is obvious. "She enjoyed being in job, for the atmosphere there was very congenial for working".(Kapur, 1972, 138)

These images of women who feel or do not feel satisfaction in their work have started appearing specially in the novels by women writers. However, they appear still in a sketchy from because romance and sentiment continue to be the main concerns. Mara of **Storm in Chandigarh** (1969) who runs a kindergarten all on her own comes alive. Mara certainly finds happiness and occupation in her school. Bold and free and westernized, she needs this work to spend her dynamic energy, but she also needs an understanding husband like Jit who helps her to come to terms with herself. In **A Backward Place** (1965) by Jhabvala, Judy who works at the Cultural Dias is happy in her work but unhappy about the social and family conditions. The writer portrays her convincingly in all situations. She is not very happy in her Indian family and social conditions but she is so mild by nature that her only act of expressing her dissatisfaction is to visit Etta and admire her fashionable style of living. She listens sympathetically to Sudhir's, her colleague's complaints, because she knows he is unhappy. In Judy we find a woman convincing in her work as rarely before in Indo-Anglian novels. Judy is an English women adjusting herself to Indian conditions in Delhi. **Bye-Bye Blackbird** (1971) by Anita Desai also has a convincing portrait in Sarah. Sarah had married an Indian but wished to keep her Indian association a secret in the place where she worked as the Head's Secretary at a school. She had a quick quality of humour but because of the marriage she had become a high-strung nervous creature, unsure of herself in white society to which she felt she could not now belong. So as she hurried along the streets children teased her – "Hurry, hurry, Mrs Scurry". (Desai, 1971, 37-38) She suspected it was Mrs. Curry. Then, in the midst of her mechanical office work a child asked, "Have you any of those Indian stamps to give me, man?" (Desai,

1971, 38) She felt her secret burst open. Her pitiable efforts to keep away the talk from her Indian husband during the tea-break gives a vivid picture if a women working under stress. Instead of a revolt there is a pitiable attempt to escape, to hide, to be unnoticed. To Judy the place of work appears comparatively better than home, but to Sarah the place of work is an ordeal. Both are midway between traditional submission and total rebellion. They are weak like Savitri in **The Dark Room**. Instead of revolt there is a pitiable hankering to be elite as in Judy's case or to be at peace as in the case of Sarah.

We find working women in the middle class-teachers, nurses, secretaries - have begun to appear in Indo-Anglian novels. Some writers use them as a spring-board for their love-story (Malgonkar and Markandaya), others put them in the East-West context (Bhattacharya, Jhabvala, Desai, Sahgal). But reality comes limping compared to the Indian fiction in regional languages where myriad problems of the working are reflected. The rise of education among women, urbanisation, freedom of the country, rising prices all have led to the middle-class women to seek work. With economic independence and educated awareness came individual consciousness. The self-denying attitude of pride in suffering gave way to an awareness if not an assertion of her rights. This phenomenon, however, is reflected only in a few novels.It is strange that in spite of the fact that some writers of Indo-Anglian fiction limit themselves to the highly sophisticated urban circles in or around cities like Delhi, the problem of the working women and her reactions are not vividly shown. A glimpse at the 300 case studies of the working women in Delhi by Dr. Promilla Kapur in her two works **Marriage and the Working Women in India** (1970) and **Love, Marriage and Sex** (1973) shows the rise of the phenomenon of the working woman and the cluster of problems she has to face at home and at her place of work, her problems of adjustment, her suffering due to the maladjustment and the revolt in her mind. These aspects could have been reflected more intensively but most of the fiction appears to deal with the surface of sophisticated circle. The superficial treatment of the middle-class working woman is a drawback of the Indo-Anglian novels.

In the fiction of R.K. Narayan, however, seems to have caught with the times to a certain extent. The long suffering wife has given way to a woman with a mind of her own as was desired by Virginia Woolf in **A Room of One's Own**. Narayan tells Krishnan about his new novel - **The Painter of Signs.**

> Malgudi is a pretty changed Malgudi. Progress has caught up with it. The year is 1972, and a family planning centre has been opened. My hero who goes to paint a sign for the centre falls passionately in love with the young woman in charge. But her own passion is birth control and she lectures men and women quite explicitly on the subject, using charts and blackboards and what not...

S. Krishnan's interview brings out more details.

> In an early novel, **The Dark Room** (one of the finest and for some odd reason least noticed of his works), Narayan had portrayed an unforgettable picture of the long suffering Hindu wife. I mentioned the book and said that the heroine of his present novel seemed a far cry from Savitri of **The Dark Room**. Narayan agrees. "In **The Dark Room**, I was concerned with showing the utter dependence of woman on man in our society. I suppose I have moved along with the times. This girl in my new novel is quite different, not only is she not dependent on men, she actually has no use for them late independence and ability to stand by herself, I took care not to give her a name with any kind of emotional connotation". (Savitri in the earlier novel is of course named after the mythical wife to whom husband is god). " I am calling her simply Daisy. She is very strong character. All the same, when you read the novel you will find she is very feminine also, there is a conflict. That is the whole point. (Krishna, 1975, 40)

It is the sum total view. The writer has moved with the times and has shown a working woman with a strong character and mind of her own. From the suffering helpless Savitri to Bharati in **Waiting for the Mahatma** and then to Daisy in **The Painter of Waiting** for the Mahatma and then to Daisy in **The Painter of Signs,** Narayan has shown the rise of individuality in woman. In **The Guide,** Narayan has also shown a dancer with individualistic traits. This dancer, Rosie, puts aside her traditional profession to marry, but leaves her husband to come to Raju, the guide. However, it is to her art as a dancer that she is dedicated and throughout the novel she makes everything subservient to that. Neither marriage nor love counts, not even money or fame. She likes to be with artists and tries to go after perfection. In her dedication to art there is an undercurrent of sincerity. For she does not allow herself to be sold to the highest bidders nor does she remain an obedient wife within the four walls of the house. She comes to Raju because she thinks he will guide her to be a dancer. When she finds he is making use of her only to make money, she feels unhappy, thinks of her husband and finally leaves everything behind to follow her art as a dancer.

In Amla, in **Voices of the City** (1965) by Anita Desai, there is a rare image of the girl leaving her parents and coming to the city to follow the career of an artist. But Amla does not have the force of personality to be a rebel. At the most, she is a sensitive creature forced to face the complexity of modern civilization and its accompanying harshness, indifference, coldness and inability to comprehend and sympathies with an artistic temperament. But she is not the central character in the novel, there is not much scope for developing her character.

Many Indo-Anglian novels give images of the dancing girl or the prostitute. These images are found in novels as widely apart from each other as **Kanthapura, The Serpent and the Rope, The Guide, Train to Pakistan and Athawar House.** In Indian tradition, coming down from the apsaras, the profession of the artist. Even in a village like Kanthapura, which might be said to have remained unchanged, since times immemorial, we have a character like 'concubine Chinna'. She is there in the professional openly. At times the writer adds a humanization touch to the character and these' characterless' women are shown to be generous-hearted a charming. Chamia in **Inqllab** (1955) by Khwaja Ahmed Abbas brings up the boy Anwar, and Mumtaz in **Morning Face** (1968) by Mulk Raj Anand cares for Krishna, the boy-hero. These women create happiness for others and seem reconciled to their lot. Their pitiable condition is stressed in some novels. Janaki in **The Big Heart** (1945) was a widow, then Ananta's mistress. She suffered from tuberculosis and Ananta, the man of big heart, felt pity and love for her. She was calm and of a loving nature. It was after her Ananta's death that she found herself cornered in her room with the police waiting outside, licking their lips like wolves, so to say, to be the first to enjoy her. It was that a cry was wrong out of her, 'No one knows what a woman suffers. How much she has to bear, silently and without protest, the abuse and the condemnation'.(Anand,1945,22)

The cry of Janaki was not a voice in the wilderness only because there was the poet, Ananta'a friend who comforted and persuaded her to live a life dedicated to the poor and downtrodden sisters. She follows him to the temple to help the woman and with his help comes out of her sorrowful plight and goes to help her sisters. Mulk Raj Anand combines reality with the ideal he has in mind for a downtrodden woman.

In Khushwant Singh's novels some pictures of women are grim, penetrating and unforgettable showing how innocence is pushed into this most ancient and ignoble of professions. **Train to Pakistan** (1956), with a terrifying sense of reality, shows the plight of a young girl budding into womanhood, being pushed by an old hag into arms of Hukamchand, a drunken magistrate, who is old enough to be her father. This Hukamchand who protests to the inspector, "We Hindus never raise our hands to strike women, but these Muslims have no respect for the weaker sex."

(Singh,1967,19) And asks him -"Have you made any arrangement for the evening?" (Singh, 1967, 21) The arrangement, of course, is for wine and woman. When this young girl, a virgin, is brought before him a thought crosses his mind that she is younger than his daughter. Yet he tells her to sing, orders others to leave. His advances to the girl, who is nonplussed, create a feeling of disgust. The girl is helpless; "she covered her face with the loose and of her sari and turned it sideways to avoid his breath". (Singh,1967,28) The whole situation is replete with pity and irony.

Mr. Singh uses broad humour to show a servant woman Shanno going to a fakir for a cure for her vague ailment, getting sexual satisfaction and becoming genial towards the servant-boy at home in **I Shall Not Hear the Nightingales** (1961). As the woman is above forty-five and a willing partner, she is put in the light of humour mixed with mild sarcasm. Shanno is not a professional prostitute; nor is she by nature a profligate woman. It is her gullibility and her desires which she can neither comprehend nor control which lead to her willing surrender to the fakir's lecherousness. She does not know why she is so cantankerous with Mundoo the servant-boy or why she maligns other young women of the family she serves or why suddenly she becomes wild. It is indolent eroticism that makes Champak to go after sex out of marriage. It is the malaise of the 'civilized lady' as in the case of Laxmi in **The Serpent and the Rope** (1960).

The prostitute of the woman of easy morals in R.K. Narayan, invariably, has associations with art and evil. She rebels against the marriage conditions or influences men to break the normal marriage code. She is a channel to waywardness but invariably has artistic talents and charm. Because of Rosie in **The Guide** (1959), Raju is lured away from his mother who calls her a snake-woman. Shanta in **Mr Sampath** (1949) lures Mr. Sampath away and Mrs Sampath has to suffer on account of her husband's infatuation. Even Bau runs after flippant girls in **The Financial Expert** (1952) while his wife suffers in silence. Every time the writer throws light on the suffering of the wife. Shantabai, in **The Dark Room**, has poetry and a bit of musical talent at her command accompanied by a certain charm to lure Ramani to such an extent that he ceases to care for his wife and children. Savitri's suffering, her feeble attempts at revolt are shown, and here again the stress is on Shantabai's actions which are responsible for the disharmony in Savitiri's family. If Narayan stresses the evil influence of the woman of easy morals, B. Bhattacharya stresses the plight of women and their frantic struggle to escape from the profession. In **So Many Hungers** (1947) and **He Who Rides a Tiger** (1954) we see women trapped in brothels, lured to it by food, or money, they are victims of poverty and man's greed for gold and lust. Kajoli is lured to the threshold of a brothel by a woman brothel-keeper while Lekha is actually put in it and saved in the nick of time by her father. The young, the innocent, the lovely, fail victims to the rapacity of man.

Malgonkar, in the historical romances of the image of the prostitute, as a princely appendage, is shown as an inseparable part of the lives of man. Gauri in **Combat of Shadows** (1962) is a passion-tangled woman. But in the later novels is a change. Woman is there to assuage the turmoil in man. The women who are concubines or pleasure-women in the princely circles (The Princes) are traditional figures with the ability to please man and they have no thought of revolt. They accept their lot. Zarina thinks it a favour when she is accepted as sisters by Abhay. But in **A Bend in the Ganges** (1964) Mumtaz is a solace to Debi not only on the physical but also the emotional plane. Though Malgonkar shows the pleasure-women to be satisfied with their lot, they bring unhappiness to the wives. Abhay's mother leads a life of loneliness till she revolts. Kamala hides her sorrow in silent dignity. Nana's wife suffers in silence in **The Devil's Wind** (1972), while the menfolk seek pleasure with the 'women of art'. Malgonkar has adopted the traditional image. The woman herself has no feeling of revolt.

In the novels of Kamala Markandaya, the profligates and the prostitutes appear in a mixed light of censure and sympathy. Kanthi in **Nectar in a Sieve** has musical talents, but she puts on superior airs and looks upon her husband, who lacks virility, as a dull fellow. She thinks that city-life would be better than village life. She feels herself closer to the world of the cities. She even snubs her village neighbours,

> No wonder they call us senseless peasant women, but I am not and never will be. There is no earth in my breeding. (Markandaya,1968,66)

Of course,Rukmani knew that Kunthi had fire and beauty in her and skill to use them. Janoki is more outspoken, 'she is a trollop, and is anxious only that there should be a supply of men'.(Markandaya,1968,66) However, it is because of famine and poverty that Kunthi becomes a professional prostitute. Kunthi does not feel ashamed of her fall; she is unscrupulous enough to squeeze Rukmani of the paltry portion of rice to be able to eat to lure more men. In contrast to her is Ira, Rukmani's lovely daughter who goes to the town to offer herself in order to be able to buy some food for her starving brother. She even cares for her albino child born out of her sacrifice.The world of the prostitutes in **A Silence of Desire** (1961) is in contrast to the world of the family, the one from which Dandekar comes. The world of prostitutes finds a symbol in the inflammation he has on his face, a festering ailment. This world is one of morbid desires of sex and in juxtaposition to the world of the spirit in which his wife moved. This general impression of squalor and morbidity is also found in **A Handfull of Rice** (1966), where the prostitutes are seen as a section of the city where all unhealthy elements dwell. Ravi moves about in this world when he is a vagabond but leaves it when he married Malini whom he loves. Caroline, highly individualized, is an unscrupulous and sexy woman who tries to possess Val, the village artist in **Possession** (1963) physically as well as spiritually.

While showing Kunthi and Ira as women, the writer came very near reality who went to the streets, one out of desire, the other out of innocent and noble sacrifice and had to suffer for it, but the handling of these characters is weak in comparison to the images of such women in Indian fiction. For example, in **The Beauty,** translated from Bengali by Manoj Basu, Radharani changes before our very eyes from a lovely, innocent and spirited girl into a victim of a male desires and is made an outcast. The Indo-Anglian writers are satisfied, working in context with generalized images, with stereotyped juxtapositions between the village and the city, between East and West. The Davdasis appear in two novels, **Chronicles of Kedaram** (1961) and **Waiting for the Mahatma** (1955). But in both they are there not for themselves but to expose the lecherous men who want to manipulate them as objects of the Mahatma's sympathy.

Writers of Indo-Anglian fiction have been more successful in dealing with the westernized society ladies of the urban and sophisticated circles. In Bhattacharya's **So Many Hungers** (1947) one such lady is nicknamed by Manju, and unsophisticated young wife, as Madame Bareback.

> She is swallowed up in her social snobbery and will not speak to teachers and such like but only to Imperial Officials.(Bhattacharya,1947,66)

The image of Madame Bareback is but a sketch but the society ladies of Steel Town and of Delhi, who appear in **Bhadow from Ladakh**, receive a more detailed attention. One such is Nandini's mother nicknamed by Biresh as Major General. This woman has the audacity to lecture to the Jawans on the topic of sacrifice for the nation when they are actually on their way to the front during the Chinese aggression. Her exact prototype is to be seen in the upper circle at Lohapur. 'Number Two' in the absence of 'Number One' is not a bit less ambitious. She wants to top the list of women sacrificing for the motherland. Her mind works fast. She decides to arrange a display of knitted garments and promote a donation drive. She plans to get a woman to knit for her and of course, she will attach her own name to the garment and win the first prize. She will invite a minister and, in his presence, her daughter Lotika will donate her ornaments and will steal the limelight. She will be photographed. Reports will be published. To be assured of this, she calls a reporter, plies him with biscuits and tea and gives him veiled suggestions to which unfortunately for her, he remains intentionally obtuse. But all this has a strange effect on Lotika who has been overhearing and she tells her mother that she is willing to donate her bank account along with her ornaments. But her mother has no intention of allowing her to do so,

> Who talks of cash? Who talks of your bank account that is kept in reserve to meet part of your marriage expense? Why, who talks of even of all your ornaments? .(Bhattacharya,1947,289-99)

The list of ornaments is carefully drawn up. It is her ear-rings her old fashioned bangles, her thin neck-chain given to her at the name-giving ceremony that are to be donated. To top this all, she lectures her daughter on selflessness,

> ' "Don't be selfish Lotika. Our soldiers are shedding their life-blood in the country's defense, and the fund I intended to provide them with necessaries". Sadness came into her heart. If only young people had the idealism, the selflessness, of their elders'. (Bhattacharya,1947,290)

Later, Number Two finds that the award goes to another women and that her daughter has donated not only the smaller trinkets but her valuable necklace as well. There is not much complexity in Bhattacharya's treatment of the character of Number Two, but he does show a considerable amount of skill in handling comic irony.Women novelists too have been successful in exposing the sham of society ladies. Anita Desai sees them through the disillusioned, cynic eyes of Nirode in **Voices in the City** (1965).

> What makes you go and trust society ladies? My mother used to be one in her Calcutta days, and I would not trust her further than I can spit. (Desai, 1965, 93)

Maya's mother-in-law in **Cry, the Peacock** (1968) undertakes social work, not because she really feels for the poor but because she wants to fill an inner void and keep herself busy. Mrs Jhabvala employs all her gifts for humour and irony in her treatment of the society ladies. Consider, for example, the following description of Etta looked upon as the epitome of fashion and manners.

> Etta arrived late. She came in the tiptoeing ostentatiously and making a strained face to show how quiet and careful she was being. Every one, however, heard and saw her, especially as she did not choose to sit at the back but tiptoed right to the front of the room. It took her some time to settle down, sitting then standing up again to smooth her skirt at the back, placing her handbag on the floor, shifting her chair a bit to bring it in line with her neighbour, turning round to wink and smile swiftly at friends. Everyone was now looking at her.(Jhabvala,1965,55)

Etta is, in reality, a deeply insecure woman who ultimately suffers a nervous breakdown. In **To Whom She Will** (1955) Jhabvala is concerned with the change of values in the post-independence period. To wear Khaddar and have a husband in prison was earlier a virtue. As Radha puts it: "Those times were quite different. Then it was honour to be poor and have nothing." (Jhabvala,1955,12)

In the post-independence period all this had changed. Patriotism had given way to a desire for money and position. So the women from the upper circles in Delhi are seen to run after money, position and western fashion. Prema, Hari's eldest sister roads sentimental novels. Amrita dreams of romantic love-marriage. Similarly in **The Nature of Passion** (1956) Nimmie's newly rich father wants his daughters to enter fashionable society. So he sends Nimmie to college and allows her a lot of freedom. She makes friends with girls whose relatives are foreign returned. She moves about with a Parsi thinking he will help her to be a member of the elite club. She even cuts her hair to appear fashionable. Nimmie is made such by her newly-rich father while the mother scolds her. Kanta, their daughter-in-law, has an attitude of secret scorn towards her in-laws who, she thinks, are not cultured enough. But she fawns on the boss whom she knows she has to please for getting a promotion for her husband. She too thinks that introducing Nimmie into high society will enhance her own prestige. So she undertakes coaching her. These characters appear again in a slightly changed form in **Esmond in India** (1958). Here it is Shakuntala, the educated daughter of rich parents, who falls in love for Esmond. Shakuntala like Nimmie and other young girls in rich families in Jhabvala's novels, runs after the thrill of romance for a while but ultimately reconciles herself to the idea of settling down to a comfortable, arranged marriage.

Jhabvala deals with the society which in her novels is the upper class society of Delhi. It is with a comic and objective view that the writer reveals the reality, the lack of sound values. The women patriots of yesterday are no more. There are only female snobs who aspire to be society ladies and go after everything that comes from the West. The elder society ladies have always an eye on material benefits. The young girls run after romance but soon come round to arranged marriages of material comfort. Dr. Radhakrishnan has pointed out that, as the women have moved into society, Western ideas have fast corroded the old moral code. Marriages are breaking and society is in a flux. Women are faced with new situation and problems and are losing their old identity. As Dr. Radhakrishnan has said:

> It is not very modern for a man or woman who is sick of his or her partner to take another, but what is really modern is the new philosophy in justification of it... but the modern woman if I may say so, is losing her self-respect. She does not respect her own individuality and uniqueness... adventurous pursuits are leading her into conflict with her own inner nature.(Ramkrishnan,1927, 88-89).

Sahgel's novels are a mirror to these remarks. The woman who try to break away from traditions in these novels only make themselves unhappy. In **This Time of Morning** the young Leela goes to America and carries with her all the traditional ideas.

> Reverence for age was a tradition bred into one's bones. An elder was a person, you stood up to greet, and consulted on all important matters. This was not hypocrisy. It was a way of life.(Sahagal,1965,67)

Leela would not wear lipstick in the presence of Kalyan whom she respected. Yet life in America brings new things with a rush and it becomes difficult for her to resist them:

> Lipstick, dancing, going out with young men, all new and strange, had come upon her in a rush because she was pretty and in demand. She had cut off her waist length hair soon after her arrival and wore it now in a shorts wining bob, but her upbringing was not as easy to discard. At times she moved uncertainly in her American environment shrinking from some of the inevitable outcomes of freedom. She turned to Rakesh at such times as the only recognizable human being in her bewildering new world. (Sahagal, 1965, 58)

Leela finds that the Western way of life conflicted with the deep sense of vlues inherent in her. There is fascination, bewilderment, fear, shame, shock, frustration and finally pregnancy and suicide for Leela. Uma's revolt, in the same novel, springs out of boredom, the malody of affluent women. Dissatisfaction is a universal feature in **Storm in Chandigarh** (1969). Urban force hasten the process of disintegration of marriages and create dissatisfied characters till the whole novel is full of estranged couples as in John Updik's **Couples.**

As in Indian literature of different languages we have a large number of novels built around the events of history. The counterpart fiction in English has also exploited the various dimensions of Indian history, its struggle for independence, rise of modernism and its deep emotional impact on Indian life and society. **Inquilab, Kandan, The Patriot, In Transit, Chronicles of Kedaram, The Sword and Sickle, Kanthapura, Sunlight on a Broken Column, A Time to be Happy, Some Inner Fury** and **Waiting for the Mahatma** are among the novels, significant for one reason or the other, that cut across myriad crusts of Indian history with varying degree of artistic success. Chaman Nahal's **Azadi** and Salman Rushdie's **Midnight's Children** are the recent awarded novels which have portrayed the wide range of Indian history before and after independence. Kamala Markandaya's **The Golden Honeycomb** lacks the range and breath of these two novels but it is a fascinating and authentic fictional articulation of a significant segment of Indian history. It can be compared with Mulk Raj Anand's **Private Life of an Indian Prince** and Manohar Malgonkar's **The Princes** more meaningfully because all these three novels explore the history of princely states in India in all their ramifications. Markandays's novel, more successfully than Anand's and Malgonkar's, juxtaposes the life of prince, his loyalty to the British rule against the life of the Indian subjects, their social awakening and cultural change. Thus behind the authenticity of experience, objectiveity of portrayal and camera-fidelity of orientation, we can discern the consciousness of dual cultures in Kamala Markandaya. The shaping spirit of cultural dualism works in this novel wrapped in the forces of history, tradition and modernity.

In **The Goldern Honeycomb** Kamala Markandaya portrays the traditional Indian society which is fast changing, and in the process shows her awareness of national awakening. Human being in their social environment have been portrayed in a state of constant change. The prominent quality of her writing is the traditional continuity at the cultural level amidst the ever-changing political; economic, and social scenes in our country. Culture to her is an idea which unites thousands of persons together and makes each of them aware of his or her integral selfhood. She explores human mind saturated with complex cultural values and records the process of development of individual consciousness. The pompous, showy and colourful life of Indian princes of which Mulk Raj Anand wrote **Private Life of an Indian Prince** (1953), and Manohar Malgonkar **The Princess** (1963) attracted Kamala Markandaya whose magnum opus **The Golden Honeycomb** was published in 1977. **The Golden Honeycomb** creates a lively description of the relationship between the British and the Indian princes, and the resultant complexities. A historical sense, a quality of tradition is created by deliberating the events that occurred in Devapur for three generations. At the same time, the vagaries and vicissitudes influencing various spheres of life have been given equal attention. The continuing but changing values of Indian portrayed in her fiction have been commented upon by A.V.Krishna Rao:

"She is equally convincing in her affirmation of the élan vital of Indian tradition, while recording in a coolly detached way the temporal and secular changes in India.(Rao,1984,3)

The Golden Honeycomb, symbolically, suggest the customary British and princely exploration of the Indians, and the consequent revolt. Bawajiraj is the drone or bumblebee and his hive is Devapur. The subjects of the State are like worker bees who furnish honey for the children of the queen bee. This implies that British and princely intrigues and trickeries honeycomb the golden State of Devapur in the pre-independence era. The golden honey is enjoyed by the British, but the bees who are subjects of Devapur, revolt against it. Consequently, the predators run away handing over the honeycomb to the native bees. It sums up the ordeals that India faced during the British dominated protest in Gandhian style. The novel, divided into three parts, each of which begins with an epigraph, starts with a prologue and ends with an epilogue, a note and acknowledgement. These appendages highlight the choice of a by-gone period of the traditional princely era and the tense national atmosphere culminating in Independence of India. The prologue points out the importance of the British-possessed Indian territory and their aim to strengthen it after America became free in 1776. In Parliament Lord Randolph Churchill pronounced :

> To watch with the most sedulous attention, to develop with most anxious care, to guard with the most united and undying resolution, the land and the people of Hindustan, that most tuly bright and precious gem in the crown of the Queen.(Markandaya,1977,ix)

The British compelled the Indian princes to accept their supremacy in India. Treaty arrangements between the princes and the British came into being. Gradually the princely States came under the British control,a the process was instrumental in bringing about the subservience of the then Indian Maharajas. Consequently the princes became alienated from the welfare of their subjects. Despite this fact, the princes were allowed to participate in various private as well as public affairs, and some of them cared much from the upliftment of their subjects. After this background information, the novelist presents deftly developed main plot of the novel dealing with Bawajiraj-III, his family, his concubine Mohini, and his son Rabindranath: and two sub-plots involving the story of Dewans and his family and the story of the Agent and Resident respectively. The development of these three beautifully woven plots coincides with the development of modern democratic movement against princely tradition. Bawajiraj-I, the popular ruler of Devapur, an imaginary princely State, embodying the spirit of independence, has been acting against the British, and hence, is dethroned and confined to prison. In the opening scene, the Baina aspirant to the throne is rejected because only a person belonging to the princely caste can be a Maharaja. The British Agent and the Devwan of Devapur choose a young couple - Bawajiraj-II and Manjula and make them the rulers of Devapur. Bawajiraj-II has been made the Maharaja to implement British policies, the marks of which needed puppets who could work according to their directions. Obvious of his status as a puppet, Bawajiran-II enjoys the princely life and is dominated by the Agents and the Dean.

But his wife Manjula, the spirited queen, rebels against princely custom and insists on suckling her baby (born in 1870) herself. He is persuaded by Bawajiraj-II to follow the princely way of life. Nursing a grievance in her heart she observes Bawajiraj-III growing into a greater loyalist. Bawajiraj-II dies in an accident, leaving behind Manjula who is a powerful force behind the reign of Devapur and his son, Bawajiraj-III who becomes the next Maharaja. In due course, Bawajiraj-III marries Shanta Devi, a princess, who bears four daughters to him. Following the princely tradition, he makes an ordinary woman Mohini his concubine. Mohini bears him a son Rabindranath, but refused to be his second Maharani. Patronized by the Dowager Maharani, Manjula, she is willing to remain his concubine and wants to bring up her son as per her own desire. Bawajiraj-III, like his father, has been taught by English tutors, has gone through the Chief's College and training in the Military Academy. He has imbibed the virtues of British administration and has become alienated from his family and his subjects. Perfectly loyal to the British, his position is like a puppet in the hands of British paramountey. Although he realizes the irrationality of the increasing levies and the sufferings of the people, yet he is in no condition to alleviate their miseries. Now and then he overlooks these matters by pretending to be a follower of his predecessors, his traditional prestige and promise. On this pretext, he rebukes the Dewan who dares to remind him to his princely responsibilities.

Rabindernath, as against the European education of his father and grandfather, is taught by a Pundit, his tutor, by Mohini and Manjula about the glorious past of the land and the heroic virtues of his ancestors. He comes to know about the world outside his palacial surroundings through his friends Janki and Das who are commoners. Gradually he imbibes the virtues of nationalism. His development is contrasted against his father Bawajiraj-III. He respects the Dewan, but oppose the Resident. The famous Delhi Durbar (1902-03) is organized to celebrate the coronation of Kind Edward VII. The Indian princes including Bawajiraj—III are fawning and cringing to the Viceroy. Bawajiraj-III is enthusiastic, but Mohini and the Dewan are sneering. The subservience of his father before the Viceroy like a lackey is very shocking to Rabi who realizes the real status of Bawajiraj-III, the Maharaja. For receiving three Rolls-Royce cars, Bawajiraj and his family to go Bombay which is in a state of political turmoil owing to the agitations of mill workers and dockers. No one recognizes him as a Maharaja. He faces the twentieth century modernity with its complexities. The tapestry law and order situation entraps the Maharaja and his entourage, and Bawajiraj and Rabindranath are wounded in two separate event. Even after being wounded the British training of the Maharaja does not allow him to realize the reality of the situation going to spread all over India including his princely State Devapur. The return of the Maharaja to Devapur witnesses the rise of nationalism among the subjects of the State. At the outbreak of the First World War, India has to send armed forces to flight for the Allies, as also for its 'freedom'. Bawajiraj-III, due to his loyalty to the British Empire, leads a force to participate in the war goes to Europe. His bravery in the war wins him award for it. While in London, he manages to bring back Sir Arthur to Devapur to replace Mr. Buckridge in 1918.

In absence of Sir Arthur Copeland, Mr. Buckridge has been instrumental in imposing the much hated new Salt Tax on the subjects of Devapur. This has been done to meet the war expenses. Usha's play, in which the rulers are shown as monsters, is distasteful to the Resident Mr. Buckridge and the Maharaja, but Rabi and the Dewan appreciate it very much. The final scenes of the novel are suffused with the national awakening which is at its zenith. The Indians are out to oppose the British who impose heavy taxes, making life even more miserable. This opposition enters Devapur in the form of antagonism to the Maharaja who does not amend the harshness of these taxes and general exploitation, and who does not resist the activities of the Resident. Rabi is on the side of the opposed people of Devapur, and is supported by Usha, the youngest daughter of the Dewan. Rabi conscious of the people's plight, has built a dam for them. He works for this and does not celebrate his attainment of majority. Even his recognition as the heir to the throne is not of much importance to him. The people's protest supported by Rabi and Usha seems to ultimately bring out the end of the British Raj in India, and this harsh reality is ultimately realized by the Maharaja and the Resident. Mohini, Rabi an Usha triumph at last, as Indian becomes free on August 15, 1947. the entire establishment has to be adjusted according to the changed times, and this becomes clear to the Dewan and Sir Arthur Copeland, while the Maharaja yields to the public pressure.

Apparently, the story proper ends with either the non-cooperation movement of the twenties, or the salt revolution of the thirties, or with the Quit India Movement of the forties. Only the epilogue points Indian Independence and the merger of the princely States to the Indian Union. Epilogue is necessary for resolving a number of strands of the novel. The British colonial expansion which formed traditional values along with princely code vis-à-vis revolt against it has been beautifully developed through description of presentation of India as a British colony, dethroning and choosing prince as tools for the success of colonial designs, traditional princely life and deviation from it, the exploitation of the subjects of Devapur through irrational taxation like salt tax, the Dewan's rational approach to the princely attitude to the people, European education of Bawajiraj-III and imbibing the virtues of nationalism by Rabi, the twentieth century democratic modernity belittling the Maharaja in Bombay, the rise of nationalism in Maharaja's transformation accepting the demands of the subjects, the end o the British Raj and finally dissolution of princely States. **The Golden Honeycomb** follows a definite chronology in mentioning the dates and years of historically and politically significant events, holding a clean mirror to the age and revealing colonial oppression and its consequences. The incidents in the novel including epilogue and prologue, cover about ninety years. Bawajiraj-III is born in 1870 and Rabindernath in 1895. Usha is born in 1903, the year in which King Edward's Coronation Durbar was celebrated. The Maharaja participate in the First World War. The Jalliawallahbag massacre of 1919 is mentioned. The nation wise Gandian whirlwind is coincided with the political unrest sweeping over Devapur. Commenting upon the use of these incidents in the novel, Margaret P. Joseph points out:

> History is subordinated to presentation of ideas that are projected through characters and events. For instance only certain aspects of the Durbar are given a detailed description because it strips the veil of illusion from Rabi's eyes. The coronation durbar of 1911, which was even more spectacular, since George-V attended it in person, is not even mentioned. There is noticeable vagueness in the reference erupting all over the country. No reforms, acts, dates, or leader' names are specified (except for Gandhi). This is in consonance with the author's usual disinclination to tie herself down to concrete particulars. A little less ambiguity might have resulted in a little more realism. (Joseph, 1980, 90).

The novel, against the historical continuity portrays three generations each of which, more or less, is proved incorporating outdated values by the successive generation. The parallelism and contrast among the generations faction as the central theme of the novel: they present the development of national spirit for reform and independence against colonial feudal exploitation. The first generation includes the political agent, Bawajiraj-II and Manjula, Narsimha Rao and the sweeper. This generation presents the British who are out to dethroning the princes, strengthening their benevolent colonial design and attaining political supremacy over princely States. The second generation constituted by Sir Arthur Copeland, Lady Mary, Bawajiraj-III, Mohini and the second Dewan, Tirumal Rao follows the foot-steps of the first one, but there is an emergence of nationalist feelings. The third generation comprising Ravi and Usha, Janki and Sophi revolt. The national activities take a concrete form of agitations and open opposition to colonialism and feudalism. The old order changed giving place to new and the democratic forces steer clear their way into the lives of Indian people. The princely States are merged into the Indian Union with the achievement of independence.

The Golden Honeycomb is a more balanced and objective portrayal of Indian history in comparison to Mulk Raj Anand's **Private Life of an Indian Prince** and Manohar Mangonkar's **The Princes** Mr. S.P. Appaswamy makes a relevant observation in this context:

> "Kamala Markandaya's presentation of the life of the rulers of these princely states rings more true than that of either Mulk Raj Anand's version, which is highly coloured for the foreign market, or even Manohar Malgonkar's, which does show some decay rather than development and change". (JIWE, VI, 62)

Anand's novel presents Victor confronted by insurmountable modern democratic forces. Anand's criticism of the princely tradition and upholding of democratic socialism fail to carry out successfully through the weak character of Victor. Manohar Malgonkar's **The Princes** has a better protagonist in Hiroji IV who is different from the weeping Victor. He is a hundred percent he-man who wins the admiration of readers. The political conflict, the rise of new forces are presented through different characters like Hiroji, his courtiers, Abhayraj, Maharani and Kanakchand. Malgonkar is able to delineate the social changes in Indian life to a considerable extent. Kamala Mrkandaya is triumphant and more successful in comparison to them because she is able to conjure up the whole gamut of princely life, the sweeping national democratic forces and socio-cultural change in Indian societies. Markandaya keeps her orbit small than Nahal and Salman sprawling materials of historical incidents.

Kamala Markandaya is able to catch history alive because

she creates living characters and history comes out embodied in them. A novelist is not a historian who will offer us a historical document or drossier. His vision has to be projected through incidents and characters. In **The Golden Honeycomb** Kamala Markandaya has shown deep insight in the handling of situations and characters. She displays an exemplary power and understanding in grappling with an enormous situation created by Indo-British struggle. She is able to create both the round and the flat characters. The Maharaja, the Dewan, Mohini, Rabi, and Sir Authur Copeland are really memorable and well developed characters while Dowager Maharani, Shanta Devi, Janki, Mr. Buceridge, Miss Sophia, the daughters of the Dewan and many others flat characters who appear before us in patches. The characters of Bawajiraj-III, Mohini, the Dewan and Rani are three dimensional palpitating with life, embodying different ideas. Bawajiraj-III, is not merely a ruler conscious of his official duty and privileges, but also a lover of his family and subjects. In Sanskrit 'Waji' means horse. Like a horse the qualities of Bawajiraj-III are horse-loyalty, sexual prowess and physical strength. His tutor Mr. Barrington rightly describes that he is a fine horseman, an excellent shot, a first class cricketer and unrivaled at Polo. He sees his destiny as bound up with the British. Instead of willing to be free from the British rule he craves for hollow British honours and decoration and the cost of sacrificing his own freedom, a representative of the class of typical Maharaja created by the British, he fully agrees with Sir Arthur in perpetuating the British rule in Indian for benefiting the people. But this is not the whole of his character. They are individuals for whom he can sacrifice all, such as Mohini and Rabi. He respects his mother and cannot think of disobeying her. His deep attachment with Mohini and Rabi becomes clear when the two leave the palace and go out on a countryside tour for getting experience. He awaits their arrival with unstinted eagerness. On the occasion o Delhi Durbar he insists on their participation in it. He also prevails upon them to join him in Simla trip. The following extract from the novel reveals his deep love for Mohini:

> 'Ah, Mohini' he sighs again. He has taken to pleading with her; it is becoming quite an exhausting business. I beg you, will you not marry me?'
>
> 'No'.
>
> 'It would make me the happiest man alive'. 'I can make you happy without that. I have no wish to be your second wife either'. 'Can you not think of the child?' 'I often think of the child. It is previsely because I think of the child'. 'I cannot understand your objection'. 'I've explained it to you'. 'I must say I defined it difficult. Even princesses do not baulk at becoming Junior Maharanis'. 'I am not a princess'. 'You could be a queen'. 'I don't want to be your queen. I went to be free'. (Markandaya, 1977, 32)

His affectionate car for Rabi finds expression in these lines:

> 'I'm sure he's safe and sound. He says he is'. ' Safe: What does he mean? 'Naturally he means that he says'. 'He says don't worry'. Bawajiraj smacks the disreputable chit his heir has scribbled and sent. 'It is possible for a father, considering everything?' 'My love, there's no need to be upset. Rabi's not a child any more. Why can't you trust him to look after himself?' 'Leaving the hotel - running off as if he were a rickshawallah- does that inspite trust'. . (Markandaya,1977,284-85))

Mohini is another fully developed and delineated character who bears significant impact on the personality of Bawajiraj-III. He is a helpless victim to the physical charms of Mohini who loves him deeply and also tries to persuade him a recognition of the dignity of Indian independence. She does not like an unflinching loyalty to foreign rulers. Her views are also shared by her son, the Pandit and the Dewan. Maharani Majula is also on her side. All of them rally around the Maharaja to make him aware that he has extra allegiance to 'Feringhis'. Manjula also enlightens her grandson and initiates him to anti-British feelings.

The Dewan is another important character now called Tirumal Rao. He is a shrewd person completely devoted to his Maharaja and the people of his State. He can be compared with the Englishman in talent and manipulation. He inherits this quality from his father Narasimha Rao. This illustrious race of Brahmin is conscious of its intellectual superiority over others in the given surroundings. The novelist gives us a clear portrait of Tirumal Rao's father:

> The Dewan, who has an interest, which he does not declare, has also dispatched emissaries whose commissions are equally strict. His concern is to secure a union which will strengthen the realm, which by means he hopes to trim the sails of the British, whose power, he fears, has grown overweening. At the same time he has no wish to strengthen the realm to the point where he, the Dewan, is rendered a chipher. The balance to be struck is a delicate one, requiring some agility and considerable skill. Narasimha Rao does not doubt himself but he is a preoccupied man. . (Markandaya, 1977, 20)

Tirumal Rao smoothly slips into his father's shoes. He is a practical and alert chief minister who gives advice to Maharaja and Resident against the newly-levelled salt taxation. He can read the writings on the wall and thus advises the Maharaja in accordance with the changing times. He knows his duty, performs them well, supervises the civil administration of his State, its resources and revenues. The novelist who is available in the novel as the omniscient third person narrative comments:

> The Dewan appoints his ministers; but he is a shrewd man (another Brahmin; the Brahmins have collared the best brains - they have proved it can be done by a system of sufficient ingenuity and singular dedication) who is very well aware of the presence

> in the cantonment and Residency; and he chooses his men accordingly. .(Markandaya,1977,37)

With his ideas and ability he becomes a significant member of the group, of character like Mohini, Rabi and his own daughter Usha. He is a voice, a new voice of modernity. However, Rabi is the most significant character in the novel standing as a contrast against Bawajiraj-III. Born in a place, Rabi grown under the training by Punditji and develops prejudices against the British, at times against the Maharaja, although he loves his parents very much. Like his mother he feels, he is one of the commoners and mixes with them wherever he gets a chance. Maharani Manjula also shapes his mind and helps him for his attitude to some extent. He hates and detests the British who work by divide and rule policy. His anti-British attitudes leads him to realize that public responsibility is more significant than private and princely indulgence. This experience or the realization of this experience is the crux of this novel. Rabi's experiences at Delhi durbar, of Bombay strike, the occurrences outside princely Devapur, his sexual encounter with Jaya, and his participation in freedom movement separate him from princely tradition. After a meeting with Janki, Das and Jaya he understands the gulf between the exploiter and the exploited. He has observed the sufferings created by floods and droughts for the uneducated poor Indian people. He encounters three main forces. He has to oppose the British, he has to flight for the prosperity of his subjects and finally he has to throw aside the traditional princely values and has to assert his individual existence. He tells Sir Aurthur in clear terms that nobody wanted to the queen to be the empress of India and that "she became empress by conquest, the people never wanted her" .(Markandaya,1977,71) Rabi and the Maharaja are thoroughly contrasted. They are antithetical characters: 'While his father is Rabi is identified with water as he undertakes to build a dam for people'. (Dwivedi, 1984,215)

He begins to take a leading role in mass struggle for India's freedom. In truth, his command over the people is complete and genuine. The Bombay strike of mill workers and dockers fizzle out because he did not have the fire for independence of the country. The masses had not become conscious of their power and co-operation. The novelist makes a revealing comment:

> This crowd is not going to make the mistake of the mill crowd, or other corwd, or any other crowd, or strike. It has discovered muscle. Further, it has found out that muscle is a mesh of physical and mental fibre. It intends to use this strength which is founded, even more basically, on its human spirit.It intends to say. If, or, if not, its heirs and successors. Time is on its side. .(Markandaya,1977,46)

Actually, Rabi is a symbol of modernity, a metaphor of new democratic socialistic forces. He is supported in his activity by Manjula, the Maharani, his mother Mohini and the Dewan. Finally the younger daughter of the Dewan Usha joins hands with him. A.V. Krishna Rao rightly says:

> "They are at once custodians of culture and makers of history in modern India; they are not only heralds of changing tradition but also the agents of change itself".(Rao,1972,24)

The contrast between Bawajiraj III and Rabi, between Bawajiraj and Mohini, between the attitudes of the Dewan and those of residents and finally the transformation of Maharaja's attitude persuade by Manjula and the Dewan give a fictive narrative to the conflict between traditional princely Indian life and changing modern democratic forces in the wake of national independence. The anti-theatrical balancing of characters does not merely make clear the conflict between tradition and modernity, it gives the novel a congruent structure. The antithetical narrative structure catches the multiplicity of history, its colourful complex spheres and also the slow but gradual cultural change. To tell the truth, Markandaya's deep and long acquaintance with the West and the East helps her hover over the novel almost invisibly in portraying characters and incidents with objectivity and candour. The duality in consciousness of culture gives a proper tenor to the conflict in tradition and modernity which is the central theme in the novel.

Kamala Markandaya's **The Golden Honeycomb** can be compared with Mulk Raj Anand's **Private Life of an Indian Prince** and Manohar Malgonkar's **The Princes** illustrate that all these three novelist articulate the area of their consciousness, the full awareness of dual cultures through their understanding of tradition and modernity. Despite the fact that Anand attempts to analyze the protagonist's psyche, the main objective of the novelist is to portray Victor, an Indian prince, who is confronted by the democratic forces. In the process Anand criticizes princely tradition and upholds democratic socialism. The encounter between tradition and modernity in the post-independence Indian presented itself with new dimensions such as cultural, political, social and psychological. These ramifications of theme can be derived by analyzing Victor's complex personality, Ganga Devi's influence over him, the relationship between Victor and his subjects, the process of the merger of his State, Maharani Indira'a appeal to the Government, and Victor's emotional entanglement with his mistress, like 'a rat in a hole'. So far as the conflict between old feudal values and new democratic ideals is concerned, the latter triumphs, dissolving the feudal tradition. People's protest and nationalist democratic movement are at war with the well established feudal State of princely order. Victor, the God in the temple of his Shamput, is replaced by the collective force of the people in whose hands lies the sovereignty of the State. Socially, Maharani Indira revolts against traditional place of woman in feudal India, and her act supports the movement for the upliftment of woman's condition. The future conflict between the inherited princely vales and the changing norms of modern society, generated by Victor's inheritance and his education on Western pattern, is easily discernible in the complex personality of the protagonist. Psychologically, the mental dilemma of a traditional public figure like Victor is that of a modern man who often finds himself in the same situation. The moral implication of Victor's psychological conflict is that that modern man should guard himself against excessive sexuality, erotic dreams and fantasises.

Malgonkar's **The Princes** attempts to portray more ambitiously the prosperous, glamorous and attractive princely India and its ruler pitched against the historical, political, social and cultural perspectives. It catches alive an important phase of Indian history when the might of the feudal princely rule was gradually disappearing at the dawn of modern democratic set-up. The decline, fall and merger of Begawad with the Indian Union represents the males is of the princely era in which common masses had to undergo tyranny, barbarity and the whim of the ruling prince. The political changes that brought about the democratic forces were acceptable to the people, but not to the prince.These turbulent forces swept away the princely order, providing the princes with privy purses and making them equivalent to ordinary citizens of India. Hiroji embodying the multi-dimensional princely tradition is thoroughly defeated by historical and political changes, by Kanakchand, and by his own Maharani whose revolt against feudal tradition is a flamboyant example of the self-defeating princely way of life. Despite the fact that the novel only deals with traditional and conservative values it cannot remain devoid of the onward march of modernity with its historical, political, social an cultural ramification. Malgonker does succeed - with consummate objectivity - in criticizing the evil aspects of both the feudal tradition a well as the corrupt politicians and modern democratic set-up. The inescapable conclusion in the **The Princes** does not present the theme of traditional princely values gradually being encroached. upon by the oncoming democratic modernity during the period of tradition.

Cpmpared to **The Princes** and **The Private, The Golden Honeycomb** is a more powerful novel than **Life of an Indian Prince** because the novel presents with clarity and authenticity the various traditional values being gradually changed with the dawn of modernity. The theme of the novel is based.

on India, especially Devapur feudal, colonial and modern. The political supremacy of the British colonizers over the Maharajas of Devapur making them wag their tails before the colonial representatives, and consequent exploitation of the poor subjects of the State are the main cause of the gradual rise of nationalism and the will for independence in consciousness of the masses. The political conflict between the ruler and the ruled leads to the socio-economic exploitation at various levels. The changing value at social-economic level cause revolt among the subjects, which triumph at last. The changing patterns of democratic modernity, prominent deviation from the norms of princely social tradition, dissolving of the caste system, the end of traditional families, and the failure of conventional princely marriages are in the atmosphere of Devapur. Taken as a whole Markandaya powerfully portrays the triumph of modernity in the political, cultural, social, and economic set-up of hitherto tradition bound princely Indian State. Later Indo-Anglian writers have thus exposed the sham of society ladies and explored the identity crisis in affluent classes. This is how they appear and present.

REFERENCES

1. Rao, Raja, *Kanthapura* ,Bombay: Oxford University Press, 1947.
2. Narasimhaish, C.D., *"Raja Rao's Kanthapra, Critical Essays on Indian Writing in English,* Ed. M.K.Naik et.al.Dharwad: Karnatak University, 1968.
3. Bhattacharaya, Bhabani, *Shadow from Ladakh* London: W.R. Allen, 1967.
4. Kapur, Promilla, *Marriage and the Working Women in India,* Bombay: Vikas Publication, 1972.
5. Malgonkar, Manohar, *Combet of Shadows,*London: Hamish Hamilton, 1963.
6. Amur, G.S., *Manohar Malgonkar,* New Delhi: Arnold-heinemann Publishers, 1973.
7. Malgonkar, Manohar, *The Princes,* London, Hamish Hamilton, 1963.

8. Desai, Anita, *Bye-Bye Blackbird,*Delhi, Hind Pocket Books, 1971.
9. Krishnan, S., *"A Day with R.K. Narayan"*, Span (Vol.XVI, No.4, April 1975), p. 40, 1975.
10. Anand, Mulk Raj, *The Big Heart*, Bombay: Kutub Popular Publications, 1945.
11. Singh, Khushwant, *Train To Pakistan*, Bombay: Pearl Publications, 1967.
12. Markandaya, Kamala, *Nectar in a Sieve,* New Delhi: Sagar Publications, 1968.
13. Bhattacharya, Bhabani, *So Many Hungers,* Bombay: Hind Kitab Publications, 1947.
14. Desai, Anita, *Voices in the City,* London: Peter Owen, 1965.
15. Jhebvala, Ruth Prawer, *A Backward Place,* Delhi, Hind Pocket Books, 1965.
16. Jhebvala, Ruth Prawer, *To Whom She Will,* London: George Allen & Unwin, 1955.
17. Radhakrishnan, S., *The Hindu View of Life,* London: George Allen & Unwin, 1927.
18. Sehgal, Nayantara, *This Time of Morning,*Delhi: Hind Pocket Books, 1965.
19. A.V. Krishna Rao, "Continuity and Change in the Novels of Kamala Markandaya" in Perspectives on Kamala Markandaya, ed. by Madhusudan Prasad, Vimal Prakashan, Ghaziabad, 1984, p. 3.
20. Desai, A., *The Golden Honeycomb,* B.I. Publication, New Delhi, 1977.
21. Joseph, Margaret P., Kamala Markandaya, Arnold Heinemann, New Delhi, 1980.
22. The Journal of Indian Writings in English, Vol.VI, Gulbarga, p. 62.
23. Dwivedi, A. N., *The Golden Honeycomb: Perspectives on Kamala Markandaya,* ed. by M. Prasad, Vimal Prakashan, Ghaziabad, 1984.

4

Diasporic Dilemmas of the Subaltern

Kamala Markandaya always feels for woman and finds her trapped in the world of men, whether in the East or West. R.K. Narayan, too, who remains anchored to his Malgudi and has been least exposed to European culture, has also included in the fabric of his novels the changes caused by Western education and culture in Indian subcontinent; these changes are depicted in the treatment of female characters Narayan observes:

> Society presses upon us all the time. The progress of the last half century may be described as the progress of the Frog out of his well. All means of communication, all methods of speedy travel, all newspapers, broadcast and every kind of invention is calculated to keep up a barrage of attack on the Frog in the well. He will not be left alone. (Narayan, 1965, 8)

Undoubtedly, the Western values and ideas have gradually but deeply moulded the life of people in India. Modernization, industrialization and scientific temper have seeped deep into the Indian soil. Kamala Markandaya, who is herself a product of the twin worlds, the native sensibility and Western knowledge, is able to give a fictional form to the flux of Indian culture with candour and concern, intensity and insight. She presents women trapped in the old world-toiling, subservient and slaving. **Nectar in a Sieve, A Silence of Desire, A Handful of Rice,** and **Two Virgins** are Kamala Markandaya's novels belonging to different phases which configurate her perception of Indian reality through the themes of tradition and modernity, representative Indian spiritual outlook and growing rational attitude. This crystallizes mostly in the female characters of Markandayas. **Nectar in a Sieve** is essentially a novel on the peasants' life, their toil, their torture, their sufferings, their tragedy but it also shows the emergence of the modern urban industrial life and its sinister consequences. It has been compared with Pearl Puck's **The Good Earth** and Bhabani Bhatacharya's **So Many Hungers**. It may even be compared with Premchand's **Godan** and **Rangbhumi.** The comparison is valid to a great extent because all these novels are shorter epics of life at grassroots. They give a full view of village world where the peasants grow and live, suffer and endure. Rukmani and Nathan are individuals they are also symbols of teeming millions. Rukmani is the daughter of a village headman whose power gradually dwindles into insignificance and she is married to a tenant farmer who is poor but warm and full of deep care for her. Rukmani is a heroic protagonist who makes a heaven out of the ordinary surroundings. She spends her day watching the seeds split, shoots break through and fruits ripen. And then things change in their life. The change came blasting in their lives, in the form of tannery, a symbol of industrialization, in the form of flood and drought, Nature red in tooth and claw. The octopus of hunger raises its ugly head and it envelops the peace and joy of their life. The important thing is to eat, to save one's life. One by one her sons join the tannery. The tannery, a symbol of mechanical power, destroys the traditional village. Rukmani's husband likes to see the sons beside him, to teach them the ways of the earth, how to sow, transplant and reap. Now he helplessly watches his sons getting employed in the tannery. The eldest son Arjun joins the tannery, the next brother followed in and left for Shillong. The third son goes out of the city to serve as a servant. In Nathan's helplessness we find the expression of the traditional Indian rural folk caught in the inevitable sweep of urbanization and industry. Yet they had to starve. The rains failed creating cracks on the earth and erasing traces of plants from the soil:

> Thereafter we fed on whatever we could find: the soft ripe fruit of the prickly year; a sweet-potato or two, blackened and half-rotten, thrown away by some more prosperous hand; sometimes a crab that Nathan managed to catch her river.... And for every edible plant or root there was a struggle a desperate competition that made enemies of friends and put an end to humanity. (Markandaya, 1986, 7)

The next son, Raja, dies and Ira, their daughter, sells her body to feed her brother Kuti. The encounter between Nathan, the father and Ira, the daughter, is poignant enough to send shiver into one's heart:

> Nathan was groping for words, stubling a little ever them. 'I will not have it said - I will not have you parading at night - Tonight and tomorrow and every night' - long as there is need. I will not hunger any more. (Markandaya, 1986, 99)

At the end of the day, Rukmani and Nathan are denied even the land they tilled. They shift to a city and work as stonebreakers in a quarry. Nathan dies under the strain and Rukmani returns with Puli, the labourer, she has adopted as her son. Nathan and Rukmani were the children of the soil and when thrown out of the soil, they lost their life. Nathan dies and Rukmani returns. She is a heroic figure who could claim like Hardy's Henchard that her sufferings were not greater than she could endure. In essence, **Nectar in a Sieve** emerges as a tragedy that exalts human dignity to a new height and shows the stuff. Apart from the Indian woman is made of dignity and endurance of human beings, the novel also explores the theme of modernity in the guise of urbanization and industry. In a sense, the essential problem of the novel is what Rukmani herself asserts:

> Somehow, I had always felt the tannery would eventually be our undoing. I had known it since the day the carts had come with their loads of bricks and noisy dusty men, staiñing the clean soft greens that had once coloured our village and cleaving its cool silence with clamour.... It had changed the face of our village beyond recognition and altered the lives of its inhabitants in a myriad ways. (Markandaya, 1986, 133-34)

The real evil is Tannery the Satan in the Garden of Eden that destroys the bliss of peasant's life. Industry was the first gift of the Western knowledge and culture. Though it was necessary for the development of a nation, yet it was the first assault on the innocence of Indian life, the simplicity of Indian people. The urban world of tannery is the world of science, industry and technology. Tannery is the 'sordid boon' about which Wordsworth laments in his sonnet **The World is Too Much with Us**. Wordsworth's fear of the loss of innocence and human potentialities becomes more explicit in the last parts of **The Prelude**. Wordsworth's predictions have come true and the whole West is now spiritually sterile. Technology ha atrophied human elements. Man is now a lonely, alienated creature living as an island unto himself. Nathan's death in the city is a poignant symbol of the truth that Indian life is also afflicted with the terror of technology. In the march of human of civilization, no country can afford to insulate itself from the contemporary scientific spirit but in its wake the innocence and vitality of Indian tradition and heritage will be affected. The encounter between tradition and change is the reality of every developing country. India is also passing through this transition. Kamala Markandaya presents the seriousness of the situation in a nascent but effective form in her first novel. This theme of modernity which is both assimilated and rejected in the culture of modern India becomes the central experience in the novel

A Silence of Desire. Something that comes out most clearly both in **Nectar in a Sieve** and **A Silence of Desire** is the determination and resilience of Indian women.

Spiritual faith is built around **A silence of Desire** which is the intrinsic ingredient of Indian life, and scepticism which is a fall out of Westernization. The women are stronger because it is the story of Dandekar and his wife both of whom represent diverse views of life - one drawing deeply from the past, another emerging from the new and contemporary. The interaction of the West and the East has resulted in the dual cultural situation. In all developing courtiers the cultural impact of the West has come to mingle and clash with the native tradition. In Indian life also we find a constant interaction between the gifts of the West and our heritage. Markandaya mirrors this reality in her novels. Sorokin, the German sociologist, explains the dynamics of cultural change with the concept of three kinds of culture, sensate, ideational and ideal. The sensate culture emphasized the role of material development and discards a belief in the spiritual and mystical aspects of life. It glorifies material pursuit and pleasure. Ideal culture, on the other hand, stresses a belief in the finer, subtler qualities of life it includes spiritual faith as a compulsive condition of human reality. Ideational culture is a stage which combines some the qualities from both. Every culture has a tendency to move from one point, one phase to the last phase and then it reverses to its original phase passing through the middle stage of ideational culture. The European world is a blossom of sensate culture and the traditional Indian culture is a gift of the ideational. Modern India faces the dilemma of passing from innocence to experience. It has to accept boons of the sensate culture and along with them their sinister consequences. A.V. Krishna Rao rightly remarks:

> In her third novel, **A Silence of Desire**, Markandaya's diagrammatical representation of the contemporary consciousness shows up a new dimension of sensibility in that the fictional focus is on the

> psychological adjustment of an urban middle class family. It is essentially a spiritual crisis for Sarojini. (Prasad, 1984, 7)

Dramatization of the conflict between faith and reason is through the life of Dandekar and his wife Sarojini and the fictional milieu they inhabit. Dandekar is a senior clerk living comfortably with his wife and three children. The opening parts of the novel give us a picture of the happy and loving domestic life which is sustained by love and efficiency of Sarojini, a good mother, wife and housekeeper. The cubit of domestic life has perfect symmetry which will gradually break and in its fold we find the macrocosmic conflict between spiritual faith and skeptical rationalism. The early part shows Dandekar as a man with joy and anticipation. Sarojini, his wife, is a centre of love and happiness.

> She was a good wife, Sarojini good with the children, and excellent cook, and efficient manager of his household, a woman who still gave him pleasure after fifteen years of marriage, less from the warmth of her responses than from her unfailing acquiescence to his demands. He was lucky.... For instance, now that she had heard his step in the courtyard she would be putting the potatoes into fry. The agreeable hiss would last until he had washed and changed and by then she would be ready for him, and so would the evening meal. (Markadaya, 1968, 7)

There is a fundamental fissure behind this smooth placid structure of appearance. Sarojini's attitude of religion is much different from that of Dandekar, and religion occupies the central place in Sarojni's life. This lack of real contact between them or sharing of the way of life between them is implicit in the beginning. Markandaya's treatment of marriage comes out from the accepted role of husband and wife in a traditional Brahmin household in which both have their distinctive places and they are aware of them. The virtues of the traditional wife are recalled in the discussion at the office, especially in Shastri's "Benign belief that wives were faithful, virtuous creature, prepared like their classical sisters to follow their husband's barefoot in jungle". (Markandaya, 1968, 23) That Sarojini's religion is deep and active is reflected by the dining room which is full of the rich prints of gods and goddesses, singly and in groups, holding courts in heavens. We must assume that to Sarojini, they are vivid presences, the guardians of her faith. On the other hand, Dandekar is not bale to describe a single god or goddess in detail even though they are parts of his background. His faith is not as developed as that of Sarojini. He has made compromises with the spreading rationalism. The difference in the attitude of Dandekar and Sarojini is not only obvious, it is significant also and it leads to the intense tension that permeates into their life. Sarojini is a woman of faith and worship, Dandekar is a man of rational explanation. The description of Dandekar's house ends with a reference to **Tulsi** that his wife worshipped. Dandekar's attitude to it is skeptical:

> Dandekar did not pray to it, he was always careful to say; it was a plant; one did not worship plants; but it was a symbol of God whom one worshipped and it was necessary that God should have symbols since no man had the power or temerity to visualize Him. (Markandaya, 1968, 5)

Here Tulsi is a symbol of God and divinity as it is in Naipaul's **The House of Mr. Billy Biswas**. Dandekar feels that Sarojini goes too far. Dandekar, however, conceals that there should be difference between God and his symbol. The difference in their attitude to religion defines their character and also acts as a thrust to the development of the story. Sarojini absents herself from the house and speaks lies:

> The girls, 'he said' have they eaten already'? 'yes. That is to say no, said Sarojini. 'I have them money to buy tiffin they will not want anything more;
>
> 'Money for tiffin', repeated Dandekar 'It seems as if you know you would have to wait so long for a bus'. (Markandaya, 1968, 16)

Curiousity comes up in the mind of readers and a sense of suspicion about Sarojini arises, but initially Dandekar has no such feelings. When he comes to know from Rajan that Sarojini has not visited her, the seeds of doubt are sown: "something remained, of troubling an elusive as minutest grit in the eye". (Markandaya, 1968, 12) Dandekar's mind is now under the grip of the *enduring tension.* His home and office turn into two areas of his mind:

> His worries over children's illnesses, the intractability of servants, relatives, insufferableness he usually forgot in office routine or they were diminished in the greater wces of his colleagues. Or if he had suffered harshness or injustice in the office, Sarojini's indignation, the extra comfort with which she took care to surround him, soon put things in their proper perspective. (Markandaya, 1968, 63)

The contemporary Indian society is reflected in Dandekar's office which shows cultural heterogeneity. People differ as individuals, but more fundamentally they are separated by cultural types. Charl is possessed with humanity and understanding. Sastri shares his feelings with Dandekar. Consequently Sastri is able to understand the internal disturbance that rages Dandekar. They share a common cultural matrix and thus they have an inkling about Sarojini's condition:

> They were talking meaninglessly, exchanging words like coins which they both knew to be counterfeit, while their minds quietly fused, acknowledging one to the other that both knew something was very wrong with Sarojini. (Markandaya, 1968, 52)

But, Ghose, Charl's deputy, a Bengali, with an M.A., from Calcutta University and a degree from Cambrigdge is an alien in this soil:

> Almost a foreigner - a man from the North who spoke differently and thought differently from the clerks, most of whom were southerners. Dandekar

> did not like foreigners - after all he had, and not so long ago, worked under an Englishman and harmoniously as that. Yet he would very much rather have aced Charl with his request than Ghose and only the urgency of his affairs drove him to the latter. (Markandaya, 1968, 189)

A host of characters are in the novel with varying attitudes and consequently they are symbols of cultural stages. If Sarojini is a positive image of traditional Indian life, Dandekar is a character born out of the cross currents of Eastern and Western Cultures. He is in the twilight zone where both cultures come to meet. The Western part in him finds its voice through his skepticism about religion and his belief in scientific system. Other characters like Joseph believe in free love. Mahadevan believes that no marriage is safe unless the wife is cloistered during her husbands absences. Ghose represents the new rising modern India shedding its medievalism and ushering in the progressive world. The transition is dramatized in the novel by a contrast between Wilson and Dandekar, Dandekar and Rajan:

> 'Stars? Horoscopes: Wilson turned abruptly. His words fell cold and cutting as an axe.
>
> 'Do you really think all that glory was created in order that some measly little priest can mumble in your ear how many brats your wife is going to have?
>
> Dandekar was equally outraged. 'Do you think, sir that in the universe, which is a whole in God's sight, any part could exist without influencing the others? Oceans rise and fall by the moon. He was quivering with indignation. 'Are human lives so worthless that the stars will not touch them'?
>
> Wilson did not answer. He surveyed Dandekar helplessly with that angry open scorn to which Dandekar knew he was subjecting Rajan; and Rajan's eyes were his own of that long ago night, obstinate

> and outraged as he gazed defiantly back at the Englishman. (Markandaya, 1968, 189)

The novelist is a skilful novelist and thus she makes all her characters integral parts of the fictional design. Through images of life in the office Markandaya broadens and deepens the tensions between Dandekar and Sarojini. The relationship between them undergoes greater intensity of tension. Events load to each other carrying the narrative further. Dandekar discovers a photograph in the trunk, the key to which Sarojini had earlier said she had misplaced. We watch him search through various layers, two special - occasion's saris, lengths of gold tissue, the silver, then exercise book out of which the photograph drops:

> "He picked it up, staring at the face that gazed benignly back at him, his heart thumping loudly as his mind races in mounting agitation. He did not know the man he was sure of that. He was equally sure it was not one of his wife's relatives -after fifteen years of marriage he knew the lot. A friend then? He dismissed the thought. A married woman did not have men friends who were not known to the husband, the family. One of the girl's idols perhaps - a teacher, a film actor? Well, it might be, he said to himself, while his uncompromising mind withdrew into some forbidding fastness of its own, from where it emerged later, and again and again without cease until at last he frantically repudiated the lie with which he had hoped to buy his peace. (Markandaya, 1968, 33-34)

Dandekar's mind is tense and is illustrated by his outer activities. His voice croaks when he speaks to Sarojini and he has to clear his throats many times to continue his speech. This shows the inner disturbance. At the office also his colleagues make jokes and comments. Joseph's remark, "you look as if your wife's run away and left you" has a pungent effect on him. He is in a mood of uncertainly. He decides later that it was all the office talk that has done this damage. Markandaya is a master of powerful expressions and she commends the strategy of words. Consequently we find here a skilful handling of verbal strategy that brings the reader closer to the immediate workings of his mind. This first occurs when he decides to question the maid Janki about Sarojini:

> But who on earth would gossip with that imbecile? He said to himself angrily all I'm going to do is to put a straightforward question and ask for a rational answer. But he did not feel any easier as he would prowl in search of her and when he could not find her he lost his head. (Markandaya, 1968, 44)

The stream of Dandekar's consciousness is clear in reader's mind. This is a modern device frequently used by psychological novelist like Virginia Woolf and Dorothy Richardson. This method of plunging the reader into the consciousness of the character is effective in that the reader comes to know the vacillating mood of Dandekar. He is between suspicion and belief. However, the growing suspicion takes stronger hold on him:

> He would find out where Sarojini was going or die in the attempt. Do it or die. Die of - He stopped. He could not see Sarojini. He had lost sight of her behind a group of shoppers - temporarily, he thought, but now she had vanished. He walked faster, forgetting his pen, ruthlessly pushing his way through the crowds and careless of the dark looks it earned him.(Markandaya,1968,67-68)

The first explicit confrontation takes place when Sarojini returns in the evening. Dendekar's anger and frustration which have been boiling inside now erupt:

> 'Mangoes', he cried shaking her furiously, so that what you want out for. Not for anything else.... No, oh no. Just for a little fruit like a dutiful housewife.

> Like a loving wife. Like a thirty whore-a-' 'For God's sake', her voice was colourless, sick, 'which God'? - the god of love?' (Markandaya, 1968, 70)

Nothing wrong is done by Sarojini; she has just kept the news of her going to the Swami for herself because Dendekar would not have accepted the values of Swami's feeling power. Since she is righteous, she is controlled and restrained in her reactions. Dandekar had accused her of having her m,usic teacher as lover, virtually calling her a soiled woman. Sarojini is not at all disturbed. She carries on her domestic duty quietly. The clash between the two implies the confrontation between the two cultures.

She is a legacy of tradition and therefore she is consistently, deeply orthodox in her faith, convinced of its total beneficence. On the other hand, Dendekar exposed to modern ideas, willing to accept Western culture, is prone to reject the older notations and practices of religion. He is caught between the residual power of the ancient world and newly acquired world which has yet to achieve full shape. Here lies the dilemma. Dandekar follows Sarojini secretly while she is going to Swami's place. He is confounded to find Sarojini before the Swami in a room of people. Her tension is partly relieved because his belief in his wife's conduct is reaffirmed. He whispers "if only you had told me... why could you not tell me?" she replies that he would have called her superstitious, a fool and then reasoned with her until she lost all faith. She is right in adding that his Western nation cannot explain what lies beyond reason. She is a woman with grains of faith and wisdom both. She has also developed endurance. These virtues are typical of Indian womanhood. It is a cultural type. An alien author, whether a liberal or humanist, could not have been able to give proper contours of these traits in a women's character. Since Indian culture is a part and parcel of Markandaya's life ad consciousness, she has been able to delineate such an authentic character. In her quietness, her endurance, her service and loyalty to her husband and, finally in her allegiance to the spirit of worship and faith. She comes out as a round, three dimensional Indian woman. Her contrast with Dandekar is so candidly forged out by Markandaya because she is equally aware of Western culture and its impact on Indian life and characters.

Swami is the third important character that forms the triangle of dilemma comes to us in the form. The Swami is a powerful figure in Indian life. Possessing special gift these holy men are intermediaries between humanity at large and the luminous powers. Consequently the Swami can create ambiguous responses such as respect and fear, faith and skepticism. K.R. Chandrashekaran rightly defines that "the Swami in **A Silence of Desire** occupies the most important place in that novel. He represents all the virtues of Indian sainthood, living a simple austere life end silently ministering to the hungry and seek".(Chandrsekharan,1977,330)

Swami is used in the novel **Possession** also. The Swami figures in R.K. Narayan's novel also but while in Narayan's fiction the Swami is an abstraction, vague and at times, a suspect. In him the fake-turned-Swami is a significant fictional motive. In Kamala Markandaya's fiction the Swami is always a positive character, opaque yet never a fraud or a cheat. The Swami is also a cultural type; the Swami in India has always been a persuasive and powerful dimension of Indian, particularly rural Indian life. They are a part of the collective unconscious of Indians, a product of the matrix of myth and rituals. That is why even Dandekar who is a character in transition, a character who accepts boldly the values of rationalism and scientific temper, is also in a state of helplessness in the Swami's presence. When he encounters him, he feels a kind of peace and he also feels unable to hold anything against him. This experience indirectly affirms Indian traditional belief in spiritual powers and the enlightened souls who have extra-ordinary supernatural qualities. Such spiritual characters are available in a large number of Indian novels in English. In Arun Joshi's ***The Last Labyrinth,*** the novelist juxtaposes the two different worlds of Eastern and Western culture through two sets of character.

On the one hand, there are the father, Som Bhaskar, and Dr. K. who believe in reason, industry and scientific approach to life. On the other hand, there are characters like the mother, Gita, the wife of Som Bhaskar, Gargi, the Sufi lady and Anuradha who represent traditional Indian culture. The mother believes that Krishna would cure her cancer. Gita trusts like birds and she engages herself in clenching her soul. Gargi is a Swami-like figure, a lady of spiritual powers in whose presence Som Bhaskar feels peculiar peace and quietness. She can be omnipresent, omniscient and omnipotent. She has transcended the limits of time and space. Since she partakes of the peace of God's unfathomable ocean, her presence is soothing and pacifying. Her touch works as a blem on the ailing Aftab. Her words refresh Anuradha and her look feels Som with peace. Arun Joshi has employed her as a symbol of a living proof of God's presence.

Yet the character of Swami is not a symbol of God, but he is definitely a positive symbol of peace and blessing. Consequently the presence of the Swami has a pacifying and powerful effect on different characters in different novels of Kamala Markandaya. In **Possession** Swami is the sustaining strength behind Val's creative power, and Lady Caroline always felt something beyond her understanding in the presence of the Swami. Here also when Dandekar meets the Swami he finds that he can hold nothing against him. He feels a calm and a peculiar detachment from the everyday affairs of life. He has the same feeling of rising above the body and the worries of the world in Swami's presence. K. R. S. Iyenger beautifully suggests that **A Silence of Desire** dares the invisible and the writing is competent enough to forge here and there coils to intricate suggestion that almost seem to bridge the chasm between matter and spirit, doubt and faith".(Iyenger,1983,442-443)

The Swami's world is radically different from that of Dandekar and his office associates. Dandekar lives between the two worlds-his house represents traditional Indian culture and spiritual faith while his office is a microcosmic symbol of change, modernity, skepticism and the world which has accepted the Western cultural values. The talk between Dandekar and the Swami reveals the split in his soul.

> Your possessions matter a great deal to you? The Swami spoke quietly, his eyes seemed to darken and grieve for him, for humanity, and Dandekar longed to day, passionately, No; they don't matter a pin's head. But truth drew him back.
>
> No, he said hoarsely, forcing himself to the shameful admission. They don't matter at all no, when I am sitting here with you. But they will, later, and that late is reality to me, in which I must live. He paused, licking his dry lips. You see, we are not rich people, we cannot afford to give away so much. (Iyenger,1983,105)

Dandekar tries desperately to get away from the Swami because he realizes 'our worlds not mix'. It is disastrous to try to mix them. The author avoids taking sides in the conflicts. Dandekar is helpless, and tries to restore the bliss and harmony of his domestic life. Sarojini has turned into a woman with a will of her own. Dandekar feels that the Swami cannot live always with them and thus he shows practical wisdom to stay away from a men who disrupts the simple tenor of one's daily life. To Sarojini, however, the tenor of daily life ceased to matter. She does not mind the children going hungry or dust gathering on the floor because these are insignificant matter compared with the deeper wisdom and peace she has received from the Swami. The situation reaches a deadlock. An external agency becomes necessary to resolve the crisis. Charl, the officer of Dandekar, appears as **dues ex machine**. Dandekar cries with agony:

> "She is still with me", said Dendekar, "but it's only the shell. All that's real is left with the Swami. Sometimes when I look at her I know she has even forgotten that I exist. I know in the Swami's world it is not easy to remember - I've been in it. I know the forgetfulness it brings - but I want to exist, to

> exist for her, I want my world back, my children happy, my floor swept". "Is that important too?"
>
> "Yes, yes, yes", he cried, "In the world I'm in, it's most important, all the small things are important, and I know it's small and petty, but I'm a small and petty man". (Iyenger, 1983, 197)

Now the tension takes a different shape and the private problem of Dendekar becomes a public issue. Government officials begin to enquire whether the Swami is a saint or Charlton. The people of the town split in two groups. Some complains that the Swami has enticed away his wives and daughters for his material gains. Others want him to stay because they have faith in his spiritual powers. On the official level Charl and his subordinate Ghosh represent two points of view. Charl, a local man with an instinctive understanding of the people wants to let the Swami live as he likes. Ghosh in his enthusiasm for rationality and abolition of superstition wants to prove that the Swami is a fraud. Ultimately the Swami himself solves the problem by leaving at his own choice. Sarojini agrees to go for the operation. The Swami has consented. Her operation is successful. Making his way home Dandekar finds the sudden release from all his problems. He rests under a banyan tee. The way its gnarled roots reach into the earth from spreading branches to begin new life gradually strengthening into new trunks is emblematic. The continuity to be re-established is obviously suggested. It will be pertinent to quote H.N. Williams here:

> *sense of* In some ways, like Graham Greene's novel of faith and doubt - ***The End of the Affair, A Silence of Desire*** is a subtle study of the reality of religious faith and of the opposition between man's modern quest for scientific 'truth' and technological certainty and the mystery n the inexplicable in the human condition. (Williams, 1976, 56)

A few significant points reveal deeper meaning in

the detailed, in-depth illustration of the story. First of all, Kamala Markandaya has given a candid, truthful picture of the modern Indian life without any personal prejudice. The cultural dualism, the strength of her vision, enables her to absorb different facets of Indian society. Even modern India is a paradox; it carries multitude of cultural traits taken both from our own tradition and the modern traditional characters as well as creatures of the twilight. Sarojini is a symbol of the spiritual India. She can be compared with Gita and Anuradha from Arun Joshi's novel **The Last Labyrinth.** Sarojini is a simpler character in comparison obviously because Arun Joshi is a much more sophisticated contemporary writer. But in essence Sarojini catches up the whole of our spiritual past. Dandekar's character is representative of a wider group of people living in modern Indian society. No country can accord to insulate itself against the prevailing currents of ideas. Because of its interaction with the Western world, Indian society has shed many of its traditional traits and has accepted the newer ideas. Dandekar is the product of this contemporary condition. He can also be compared with the hero Som Bhaskar of Arun Joshi's **The Last Labyrinth**. Both the characters enact the crisis of consciousness in a modern Indian man. Som Bhaskar is highly educated, widely traveled, largely experienced. He has read the Western philosophy and at the same time has shared the experience, the mystical religious experience at Banaras. He is a searcher exploring the labyrinth of life ad death, reality and truth, doubt and faith. In his quest, in his intent to unravel the cosmic mystery, "Bhaskar is a modernized, secularized, emparishized, skeptical Nechiketa who has been dented the faith and resolution of **The Upanishadic Model".**(Prasad,1985,106) Dandekar does not have metaphysical dimension of Som Bhaskar but at the social level he is also a character tossed between tradition and modernity, spiritual faith and skepticism. He is also, like Som Bhaskar, a contemporary Indian everyman because he straddles two cultures together. His dilemma is the predicament of a contemporary Indian whose roots are in his own soil but he also responds to the west wind that blows. In short, Dandekar is the creation of cultural dualism. Dandekar vacillates between doubt and faith. His modern self forces him to explain the role of the Swami rationally, but he feels a peculiar hypnotic serenity in the Swami's presence. He is transported to a new world as it were. He jerks himself into mundane reality. This twin consciousness is typically symbolic of Indian condition.

This divergence between tradition and modernity, spiritual stance and scientific spirit may also be meaningfully explained in terms of Sorokin's concept of the dynamics of cultural change. Sorokin rightly believes that the Western world has sensataculture. They are at the one end of the spectrum. At the other end of the spectrum is the ideal culture which prevailed in India in the ancient times. In process of change the culture of one country interacts with that of another and shares the traits from both. This middle phase is known as intentional culture which combines Eastern belief in religion, magic, mystery, and fine arts and the Western pragmatism, skepticism and the scientific temper. Dendekar's dilemma is the dilemma of having twin worlds in his spirit. Women seem to have no such dilemmas. Though they live in a predominantly male world, and the modes and codes governing their lives have been devised by men to suit their own needs and fancies, yet the women characters of Markandaya seem to be stronger. They represent a life of unflinching faith. Only the women who have lost their moorings in traditional Indian ways suffer from self-division. Such women are driven to despair and suicide. But to the majority of the Indian women faith provides a firm anchor; they suffer but do not break. And this is the fact that the writer wants to highlight.

Woman has been a victim : of circumstances, of crafted social designs and so on. **Nectar in a Sieve** has a character named Rukmani, the narrator-heroine, who has been described as "a mother of sorrows". Rukmani's tale of suffering affirms the value of hope and struggle: One must hope, and one must persevere even if one is engaged only in trying to discover "nectar in a sieve". But Rukmani is a generic type rather than an individual. She represents of faith, resilience and power of endurance that characterizes Indian women. She is identified with the Indian earth. Rukmani presents a study in contrast when viewed against her male counterparts. There is a lot of fight in Nathan, and Ravi of **A Handful of Rice** is neither a drifter not a shirker. But to all of them - the principal breadwinners of the family-life is extremely difficult. At times they give in to despair. But Rukmani or even young Kamala are delicate, dependent and yielding types when viewed from without. But deep within they are hard and capable of enduring a lot of suffering. It is Aunt Alemelu of **Two Virgins** who gives a clue to the understanding of the power of the long suffering. Indian women: it stems from their deep and abiding faith in the traditional Indian values. The old Aunt, always grumbling, working and fretting, is bitterly critical of the Western way of life. To her this way of life is symbolized by Miss Mendoza of the Missionary School (English education) and Mr. Gupta who represents the city and film industry. Fascinated by the glare of modernity, Lalitha wants to be a film star. Aunt Alemelu fears that Lalitha's life might be plagued by misfortune. Though rather simplistic in outline this view of life helps define some attitudes and preferences. Markandaya, for all her western education and exposure to the West has a facile understanding of the Indian women. The Indian woman is rooted in the tradition, no doubt. But how much o tradition is backwardness, and how much of it is culture, Markandaya is unable to decide. Everywhere in her world the women suffer and Kamala Markandaya tries to show the dignity and triumph of women's suffering. It is the autobiography of Rukmani, and the drama of her relentless suffering is enacted against the background of a village in tradition. Rukmani is a witness to a socio-historical process which causes the disintegration of her family. Symbolically it represents the disintegration of a way of life which Rukmani suffers in her own person. To some it stands for the disintegration of the rural way of life under the impact of modernity. Rukmani loses her home, her children, and finally she is cruelly uprooted from the land of her birth. With Rukmani and Nathan breaking stones in the alien city for their subsistence her life touches the rock bottom of misery. In **Nectar in a Sieve** we watch Rukmani, as if on the cinema-screen, from the time she came of age upto the time she returns to the village as an old widow, and is able to survey her past "with calm of mind all passion spent". She is a child of the transition between the insular, autonomous village life of old and the new village life dependent upon urban civilization and in constant contact with it. Rukmani's father is the village headman, a position that once carried much power and prestige but which now, with changing times, has lost both. As a result Rukmani's wedding was not half as colourful as her sister's had been. A bride at 12, Rukmani is a mother at 13, mother of six children at 24, old at 40. Put bluntly in this manner the graph of Rukmani's growth and decline is shocking. But Kamala Markandaya weaves the facts so evenly into the story that one sympathetically realizes that tropical flowers in their natural state blossom early, wither soon, and yet retain a lingering fragrance. Rukmani's story, despite the redeeming fragrance or dignity of suffering or whatever we may choose to call it, is in fact the pathetic story of the burdened and sorrowful womanhood of India. Rukmani and Nathan are happy together:

> "A woman, they say, remembers her wedding night.... But for me there are other nights I prefer to remember, sweeter fuller, when I went to my husband matured in mind as well as in body".(Markadaya,1955,27)

For Rukmani and Nathan this happiness is perilously threatened by factors beyond the control of Rukamani and Nathan. There is deluge, followed by severe drought. They starve, subsist on wild plants and grass, but despite all odds, manage to live on. But calamities overtake them in quick succession. Their two eldest sons leave them and go away to Ceylon, the third is killed in the factory, and another starves to death, and still another goes away to eke out a living in the city. Thus the family disintegrates. They are evicted from their land and forced to migrate to the city. Unable to trace their son in the alien, sprawling city they try to earn their bread by various means, including by breaking stones. Behind their myriad attempts at survival there is the nostalgia for their own land. They want to earn enough to pay their passage to their native village. Nathen dies in the city. But Rukmani, the stronger of the two, survives to realize her modest dream. She returns to the village where she is welcomed by her son and daughter who still live there. The travails of Rukmani are the travail of the Indian women, and by extension of the teeming millions who live in villages at the mercy of nature. The vagaries of nature determine happiness or unhappiness of the Indian farmer. Sometimes it does not rain and there is drought and he is ruined, and at other time, the rains are excessive and his crops and belongings are washed away. But even though the forces of nature or of circumstances prove stronger than man the women seem to shine forth in all their strength. Against the raging flood and an extremely uncertain future Rukmani stands firm and calm. Outside the village roads are submerged in swirling flood waters and inside the sky pours into their hut as the roof has become tattered and leaky. But Rukmani does not give up. Her most powerful resource against suffering is a belief in tomorrow. Besides, she has saved a little rice hidden away in a corner for sustaining the children in rainy days. In Rukmani's scheme of things like that of Ernest Hemingway's Old Man, Santiago ,"Man is not made for defeat. He may be destroyed but not defeated". (Hemingway,1959,96)

Such circumstances pursue Rukmani with unabated malice. She is tormented even by her own kind. Kunthi, who flourishes on blackmail, and other crooked and immoral devices is also a woman. Taking the analogy once again from Ernest Hemingway's symbolic novel, **The Old Man and the Sea** not all swimming things are like the noble and heroic marlin who fights a principled fight; there are predatory sharks too. Kunthi is a shark who has nothing but ravenous appetite and sharp teeth and who do not show grass under pressure. Kamala Markandaya who shows the struggle and nobility of women in almost all her fiction has deliberately created Kunthi who is a perversion of the values embodied by her major women characters. Kunthi is both a foil and contrast to Rukmani. Though persecuted by Kunthi Rukmani shines forth in contrast as a supervisor being who loses many precious things in the dark hours of misery, but not her faith and character. The woman, irrespective of her status, is a sustainer of life.

In **A Handful of Rice** the women like Jayamma and Nalini overshadow Ravi. They remain calm and unperturbed in the face of suffering. It also implies a co presence of tradition and modernity and an awareness of both the traditional values and new trends of the materialistic Western culture. It deals with an Indian caught in the vortex of change, a change from the rural society deeply anchored in tradition to the machine-based materialistic urban society. Like all the novels of Kamala Markandaya it derives its aesthetic validity from the interlocked polarities of religion and science, possession and renunciation, empiricism and transcendentalism".(Kumar,1968,86) Whereas **Nectar in a Sieve** is purely a novel of rural problems, depicting the poverty and hunger of the rural masses, **A Handful of Rice** deals with urban life with its struggle for survival. As Kai Nicholson rightly points out, in **A Handful of Rice**, Mrs. Markandaya "uses the village as a pretext for her hero, Ravi to flee the conuntryside and plunge into the turmoil of urban life". (Nicholson,1972,117)

If Mulk Raj Anand's Bakha in **Untouchable** is a case study of the 'thirties, Ravi the central character in **A Handful of Rice** is a proletarian product of the fifties. Belonging to the generation of 'angry youngman' who rebel against fatalistic attitude of subservience, Ravi has the initiative to fight for a proper place in society. But, he is ultimately forced by socio-economic oppression to recede back into his inherited destiny. Ravi is the son of a poor peasant in a village. A perpetual victim of poverty, he is tired of hunger. To escape from the rural poverty and hunger, he leaves his village and joins the general exodus to the city. He could see that the villagers,

> Had all lived between the genteel and acute poverty - the kind in which the weakest went to the wall, the old ones and the babies, dying of tuberculosis, dysentery, the 'felling fever ' recurrent fever', and any other names for what was basically, simply, nothing but starvation. (Nicholson,1972,25-26)

In fact the cities, like the villages, have nothing to offer poor people like Ravi, "it held out before them like an incandescent carrot the hope that one day, some day, there would be something".(Iyenger,1973,445-6) In his endeavour to save himself from starvation, Ravi faces a series of trials and tribulations and gets disillusioned. Floating through different streets in the city, he joins a gang of loafers and criminals. Initiated into the mystery of urban existence by Damodar, Ravi becomes a part of the underworld of smugglers and boot-leggers. He is exposed to the evil that rages in the city in many forms:

> The insensitiveness of the affluent, their mains for conspicuous consumption, their hardness of heart: the exploitation of small fish by the big, the worker by the capitalist, the Apu's of the world by the Big Shops in Mount Road: and the infernal success of the bootlegger, the black marketer, the drug-peddlar at the cost of the poor, the down an out, the desperate. (Markandaya,1966,198)

Ravi witnesses life in all its raw hunger, want and exploitation as a member of Damoder's coterie. He finds life in the city a fierce for survival. With its 'lawlessness' and 'darkness' the city is a jungle. Ravi realizes how "in this jungle one had to fight, fiercely, with whatever weapons one had. Or go under". (Markandaya,1966,213) However, in his earnest effort to strike roots in the city environment. Ravi finds Apu's tailoring convenient, though monotonous, falls in love with the tailor's daughter, Nalini, and decides to put an end to his criminal career. He agrees to work as an apprentice with Apu, and becomes a member of his family by marrying his daughter. The novel takes the turning point when Apu dies and Ravi becomes the head of the family. He shoulders the responsibility of the entire family only to get bogged in an atmosphere of gloom an despondency; he proves himself a misfit for the role Apu wanted him to play in that big family. His unwillingness to toe Apu's code of conduct leads to a decrease of income. And with soaring prices he has to raise loans to make both ends meet. He says, "I've borrowed on the sewing-machine, I have to keep up the interest payments... and the rent is mounting up... and the light bill.... And there's no water". (Markandaya, 1966, 213) This affects his temper also. He becomes a man of fretful nature and beats his wife. Nalini leaves the house after quarreling with him. Two of the dependents leave the house. Damodar, no doubt, is ready to help him provided he joins him in black-marketing and hoarding. But Ravi is totally opposed to the idea. Debts pile up. Life becomes miserable. His son dies of meningitis.Unemployed and desperate, Ravi approaches once again. But he is that people with 'no guts' cannot work with a person like him. Damodar advises him to "Go back to your village, it's more your size, you are not fit for anything else". (Markandaya,1966,214)With his moral indignation Ravi rose unsteadily. He felt like retching but he controlled the spasms and went down to the street". (Markandaya, 1966, 216) Thus Ravi's integrity finally alienated him. The novel comes to a close with the crowd episode. Ravi joins the hungry crowd which plunders the rice go downs in the market place rending the sky with the slogan: "Rice today, rice. Rice today, rice". (Markandaya,1966,233)He struggles and goes very close to the rice bags, but fails to get even a hand full of rice:

"He struggled to reach the grain, this time at least,

> and he clenched his empty hands and watched with frantic eyes as the rich heap dwindled, and the empty sacks flopped and sagged and were snatched up and filled or humped away full of shoulders that could bear them". (Markandaya, 1966, 235)

Again he joins the regrouped mob, indulging in looting and destruction. When his turn comes he takes a brick to hurl at the Nabob's Row, "but suddenly he could not. The strength that had inflamed him, the strength of a suppressed laminated anger, ebbed as quickly as it had risen. His hand dropped." (Markandaya,1966,237) Ravi's dilemma is essentially moral. As Margaret P. Joseph aptly remarks: "In this dichotomy between idea and fact, in the impossibility of bridging the gap between desire and honest fulfillment, lies the essence of the tragic"(Joseph,1980,62)

The plight of Ravi reminds us of some of Dickens' characters. Ravi's dependence on Damodar for survival invariably reminds us of Oliver Twist's dependence on equally crooked artful Dodger. Ravi's contact with Apu and his family which enables him to have a short period of happiness recalls David Copperfield's friendship with Dorm and the happy environment of his new home with her foster parents. Like Dickens he is not only aware of the problems of the society, he also looks at them from a moral point of view. Ravi's dilemmas is the dilemma of being caught between two values, the traditional ethical ideals and the new pragmatic rational approach. Professor K.R.S. Iyengar remarks:

> "Caught between the pull of the old tradition that all but strangles him and the pull of the new immorality that attracts as well as frightens him, Ravi lurches now this side now the other side, and has the worst of both".(Iyenger,1973,446)

We may disagree with Professor Iyengar in saying that Ravi has an experience of both; he does not have the worst of both. The ultimate triumph of conscience which puts a restraint on Ravi's anger and rebellion and makes him turn away from the crowd is an assertion of the traditional Indian cultural heritage of the purity of means and ends. In his protest and rebellion, in his existential agony he is a modern character articulating changing facets of Indian society. The changing reality of Indian life has emerged both from the new social conditions as well as an influence of the Western culture. Ravi's shift from Damodar's underworld to the poor but humane world of Apu's family and his consequent shouldering of the responsibility is a journey from dark sub-human underworld to the human world of emotion and conscience. The triumph of conscience is the triumph of traditional values. Both Ravi and Dandekar are products of cultural dualism. Dandekar's problem in **A Silence of Desire** was existential and spiritual. He wanted to exist as a common every man and thus the world of the Swami which existed on a higher plane, which pushed him towards spiritual quietness and peace was terrifying to him: "I want my world back". He wants to exist in his small world: "The world I'm in, it's most important all the small things are important". (Markandaya,1960,197)

The bliss of the spiritual and the elusive is the Swami who is the springboard of his wife's faith seems to be a threat for him, for his small world. Ravi's dilemma, on the other hand is existential pitted against the moral. He is also a common Indian everyman living his life in the urban milieu which is in a state of constant flux. The immediate situation in India after independence was not only of political uncertainty but also of cultural heterogeneity. It was almost a melting pot where traditional values, moral and spiritual, imported values of pragmatism and progress. Ravi is lured by the principle of end but finally the purity of means prevails on him. He is a symbol of the existential crisis solved through the ethical values. In his dilemma and crisis he enacts cultural dualism.

The novel **Two Virgins** is of lesser achievement both in quality of structure and clarity of experience, but this novel also presents the dilemma of Indian people who are passing through the process of change. The polarity between tradition and modernity which we have analyzed at length in her novel **A Silence of Desire** is discernible in **Two Virgins** also. Apparently this is a novel that tells us the story of a young girl who runs away to the city and ruins herself and brings disrepute on the family by running after the film career. By implication it is a novel on the conflict between the old and the new, the rural and the urban. In the process of the story we find the interaction between rural Indian cultural values and modern urban Westernized cultural impact. The novelist presents the story by juxtaposing the village against the city characters who align themselves to two opposing groups. It is the story of two sisters in an Indian village where they grow between love and conflict of the parents, fortunes and misfortunes of the family. The new irresistible material values clash against established ancient beliefs and relationship within the family and the village. The village has innocence and sustaining strength for its inhabitants. The city, on the other hand, is hostile to human innocence; it is sinister in its influences. In **A Handful of Rice** the city to which the protagonist runs and in which he spends his life is full of agony, strife, misery and vicissitude of life. In Anita Desai's **Voice in the City** Calcutta is a symbol of disaster and disinheritance. The city is not only a powerful symbol, it is the pervasive spirit that gobbles peace and harmony of the characters. In **Two Virgins** also Kamala Markandaya pits the city against the village:

> She wanted to go home. At home there were fields to rest your eyes on, colours that changed with the seasons. The tender green of new crops, the tawny shades of harvest, the tints of freshly turned earth, you could have told the week and the month of the year by these alone. You knew each grove, each acre, each homestead on it, who owned them, and the owners of the names. You knew every pathway. No one could ever be lost, not by trying. The walls, the fields, each had its name; the well beside the water meadow, the well by the banyan, the field next to the mill. You always knew where you were. You

know who you were. (Markandaya, 1977, 243)

The village and the city has a contrast between which is expressed in such passages but more than that it is engrained in the narrative of the story itself. This is further strengthened by the juxtaposing of two sets of characters. Aunt Alamelu is the most important character who represents the ancient tradition of India and wisdom of village life. Her attitude to the daughters of the family, to Miss Mendoza, the Principal of Convent School and Mr. Gupta, the film producer, indicates in most clear and palpable terms the Indian stance of life. When Miss Mendoza is to pay a visit to their house, her relations outlive her character.

> How the days fly, Amma took a saying, She usually said it at Deepavali, and when new years and birthdays came round, but now that the date of or Miss Mendoza's visit was fixed she said it almost everyday. It drove Aunt Alamelu frantic. She said she knew she was getting older minute by minute, but reminded? She was quite caustic, the truth of the matter was she disapproved of Miss Mendoza's ways, which were modern.(Markandaya,1977,57)

Her reactions to the idea of Lalitha taking part in film indicates her symbolic value,

> You want to be what? She cried. Are my ears deceiving me, can I be hearing aright? She smelled of dhal and the green chilies she had been crushing, it was a formidable smell, you heard, said Lalitha. She was insolent, stuck out her lower lip and glared at Aunt Alamelu, but it was wasted, it glanced off the hide she had developed which rivaled Chingleput's. Your, a respectable girl, a girl from a respected family, cried Aunt Alamelu, you want to be nautch girl, decadasi such as no one in our line not for twenty generations has ever descended to being, it that your ambition? (Markandaya,1977,82)

We have a typical Indian woman, Amma, quiet and submissive, co-operative and obeying to the father. Miss Mendoza and Appa represent the twilight world where Indian tradition and values are preserved but along with them they also willingly accept Western modern values. He backs his daughter Lalitha and likes Indians to be Westernized which "advanced them into the big world instead of remaining static in a back water".(Markandaya,1977,57) Amma was ambivalent; she admired Miss Mendoza for the way she ran the school, but she would not have anted her daughter to be unmarried teacher like her. Lalitha and Saroja have many similar traits as daughters of the same parents, pupils of the same school, they share common values and attitudes but there is a basic difference in their character. The difference in them reminds the readers of the difference between Elizabeth and Lydia in **Pride and Prejudice** and Elinor and Marianne in **Sense and Sensibility.** Lalitha is prettier, braver and more daring than Saroja. She has fallibility towards lures of the glamorous life of city and the film world. She has much interest in sex and mystery of sex-life. Consequently she becomes a victim of the share of a film world which is represented by Mr. Gupta. Mr. Gupta and his film world stand for the sinister influence of Western culture which has emphasized material values at the coast of tradition and heritage. Saroja also has inclinations for the glamour of the film world and the mystery of sex-life but she bears the influence of Aunt Alamelu. Alemelu ha imbued in her a respect for traditional values.This helps her preserve virginity in spite of passion and desire which surged within her. What saves her perhaps is the attitude of fear, revulsion and distrust she has developed towards the city and its people after the shock that Lalitha's example has given her. The contrast between the city and the village at the level of the landscape and among characters like Aunt Alamelu, Amma and Saroja on the one hand and Miss Mendoza, Mr. Gupta and Lalitha on the other enact an implicit tension at the level of culture.

Here the dilemma is of culture dualism manifested through the influence of urban, modern, Western cultural values creating their effect on the rural, ethical, simple traditional Indian way of life and its values. The characters and the milieu they inhabit stand for some values, some cultural patterns. Markanday's awareness of cultural dualism reveals itself quite successful through her exploration into the experience of adolescence of a girl.The conflict between tradition and modernity may also be explained in this novel by analyzing it as a novel of escape and initiation. The story of the sisters involves a series of escapes such as the adolescent "seeking escapes from the world of home and village into a wilder world, full of lure and opportunities". (Ramamurti, 1984, 203)

In this novel there is initiation into the world of modernity and Western culture. The two cultures are contoured by the contrast between the village and the city and Alamelu and Mr. Gupta. Lalitha is a victim of cultural interaction, but Saroja comes out triumphantly from the criss-cross of two cultural conditions. In contemporary Indian life the growing children are placed in this dilemma of rural simplicity and urban sophistication. On the one hand Indian culture asserts itself through its spiritual value while Western culture pulls them towards material rational values. Therefore, most of modern Indian novels written in English have articulated cultural dualism by this kind of polarity of characters and locale. Arun Joshi's **The Last Labyrinth** also enacts the dilemma of an Indian who is the product of dual cultural situations. The Western world is spelt out by Desecrate Spinoza, Fraud and Marx, the Eastern world by Benaras. In terms of character, the Mother, Anuratha, Sufi lady, Aftab and Gita give a living form to the spirit of belief, faith, mystery, religion and sacrifice. Lila Sabnis, Doctor K. and the father stand for the Western scientific rational stance of life. Bhaskar, the hero is torn between the two. He is a Hamlet reflecting over the problem to believe or not to believe. Lalitha and Saroja are simpler and inferior characters but in their own ways they also have dramatized the conflict between tradition and modernity. They are also creatures of cultural dualism.

We have a novel **Nectar in a Sieve**, which has been aptly described as a microcosm of modern India. The drama of struggle against innumerable and insuperable odds takes place in a typical Indian village. One may call the village Kamala Markandaya's Malgudi or her Kanthapura. It is symbolic of India. Rukmani and Nathan symbolize the rural masses of India. Kamala Markandaya had a first hand, intimate knowledge of the life of the rural poor, and hence her delineation of it is remarkable for its realism and penetration. In this way she has rendered the soul of India not only to the West, but also to the educated elite of India living in the cities. The setting is provided by a South Indian village, situated in the neighbourhood of a city. The name of the village and its exact locale have not been given. We can only guess that it is some village in the vicinity of Madras. The novelist has not given any name to the village, for it may be any of the myriad villages of India. The hard facts of village lie, as presented in the novel, are true of all Indian villages, whether in the south or the north. In other words, the village is a symbolic village, symbolic of rural India, and not any one village in particular. Likewise, the characters are more important representative types than individuals. Rukmani, Jayamma and Kamala represent the Indian womanhood.

It is a complex work of art, and that is why it has evoked most varied responses. Some have called it an eloquent cry of despair, while others have called it a great tragic novel in which "the terror of impersonal fate is balanced by pity and admiration for truly noble human beings. Others have interpreted it in existential terms and have pointed out that the characters in the novel have to make "choice" determines their future. There is no doubt that there is much suffering hunger and starvation, disease and death, in the novel. It is the life-story of Rukmani in her own words. The social background is provided by a village in transition, and the conflict and tensions are caused by the intrusion of modern industry. Life lived in rural Indian is the backdrop to the personal story of Rukmani and Nathan, and her suffering and the disintegration of her family face and mingle with the disintegration of the rural way of life under the impact of modernity. The flow of life in an Indian village has been realistically depicted with sympathy, understanding, and skill, and without comment. The picture of rural India thus presented in comprehensive and all embracing. We are the Indian peasant in happiness, in his pride, in his fields and crops, in his fatalism and unflinching faith in Divine Providence. We also get a realistic account of his heart-rending suffering and helplessness. He is poor and often on the verge of starvation. He is exploited by the village Banya and the landlord who insists on realizing the amount of his loan even through the crops have been completely ravaged and ruined by rains. The wicked Kunthi can manage to survive by adopting crooked and immoral ways. Driven to the edge of despair, Ira may decide to sell her body. But to those who adopt the straight course life is much more difficult. But this is not say that Kamala Markandaya has created a world full of evil, suffering and despair. There are noble souls like Dr. Kenny whose sympathies overflow the barriers of class and nationality. Dr. Kenny discovers that the passivity of the Indian masses is a great disadvantage. The suffering of the rural dwellers is accentuated as a result of the wider conflict between the agrarian and industrial way of life. Rukmani lives in such a village and the disintegration of the rural way of life under the impact of industrialization is reflected in the disintegration of her own family. The travails of Rukmani are the travails of the Kamala Markandaya's women.

The crumbling of the rural way of life leads to much suffering and uprooting. Nathen and Rukmani and others in the novel are frequently faced with the necessity of making a choice. As long as a man has his roots he lives; and he dies if he is uprooted. Exactly such uprooting is caused by industrialization. Nathan had his roots deep in his land and he lives on so long as he is not uprooted from the land. He is able to face successfully, with courage and determination, the misery and starvation caused by unprecedented rains and draught. He survives through the ordeal, would have lived on as a satisfied and happy farmer, had he not been uprooted from his land. But the tannery swallows up their land, and they are evicted an dispossessed. Nathan is forced to make a choice. He decides to go to the city to seek shelter there with his son Murugan, but this rootlessness is to him unbearable. His soul is scarred. They travel by bullock-cart to the city at a distance of a hundred miles, and their journey, and their suffering on the way, has been described in detail, for it is symbolic of similar journeys undertaken all over the country in the wake of industrialization. Nathan's roots are gone, and so like an uprooted tree he cannot live for long. He falls and dies. Similarly others in the novel have also to make 'choices' and suffer consequently as a result of the choice they make.

No doubt, there is much suffering, hunger and starvation all-round, but merely for this reason it cannot be called "a cry of despair". it would be more correct to call it an apotheosis of the human spirit, like the great tragedies of Shakespeare. It reveals the heroic grandeur, nobility and endurance of people like Nathan and Rukmani, who struggle relentlessly and heroically against an impersonal fate which seems constantly to pursue them, bent on destroying them. The working of this cruel and terrible impersonal fate, which often assumes the form of the vagaries of nature, is balanced by our admiration for the heroic grandeur and nobility of soul of such characters. Rukmani and Nathan experience the extremes of hunger and suffering, but their integrity remains intact and unshaken. Even Kunthi with all her blackmailing falls to drive a wedge between them. In the city, they have to undergo unbearable sufferings, and are driven from pillar to post, as if by the working of some relentless, hostile and impersonal, but despite all this suffering, they continue to struggle with their heads bloody with the buffets of misfortune, but unbowed.

Nathan falls a victim to this impersonal power, fate or destiny, pursuing them relentlessly, but Rukmani returns to the village, "with calm of mind all passion spent" and is welcomed by her son Selvem an her daughter Ira. Puli, her adopted son, comes with her and is adequately treated for leprosy. The hospital of Dr. Kenny has been constructed and Selvam is well-employed. He is a loving and dutiful son and we have glimpses of Rukmani living to a comfortable old age with her children.

Precisely, the novel is a realistic presentation of the suffering, hunger and starvation which is the fate of the Indian peasant even to-day. But merely for this reason it cannot be called "a cry of despair". Rather, it is a great tragic novel, an 'apotheosis of the human spirit' like all great tragedies. The experiences it narrates, and the life it depicts, are as relevant today as when it was it was penned. Rukmani, the mother of sorrows, suffers, endures and triumphs. The emphasis is not simply on her suffering but on her ability to endure and overcome. The suffering is nullified with the endurance and patience.

REFERENCES

1. Markandaya, K., *Nectar in a Sieve,* Jaico Pub. House, Bombay, 1955.
2. Hemingway, E., *The Old Man and the Sea,* Charles Scribner's New York, 1959.
3. Kumar, S. K., *"Tradition and Change in the Novels of Kamala Markandays",* Kakative Journal of English Studies, vol.III, 1968, p. 86.
4. Nicholson, K., *A Presentation of Social Problems in the Indo-Anglian and the Anglo-Indian Novel,* Jaico Publishing House, Bombay, 1972.
5. Iyenger, K.R.S., *Indian Writing in English,* Asia Publishing House, Bombay, 1973.
6. Markandaya, K., *A Hundful of Rice,* Orient Paperbacks, New Delhi, 1966.
7. Joseph, M. P., *Kamala Markandaya,* Arnold Heinemann, New Delhi, 1980.
8. Markandaya, K., *A Silence of Desire,* Four Square Books, London, 1960.

9. Markandaya, K., *Two Virgins,* Vikas Publishing House Pvt. Ltd., New Delhi, 1977.

10. Ramamurti, K.S., *"Two Virgins: A Problem Novel"* in Perspectives on Kamala Markandaya, ed. By M. Prasad, Vimal Prakashan, Ghaziabad, 1984.

11. Narayanan, R.K., *Next Sunday,* Orient Paperbacks, New Delhi, 1965.

12. Markandaya, K., *Nectar in a Sieve,* Jaico Publishing House, Bombay, 1986.

13. Prasad,M.,Ed. *"Continuity and Change" in Perspective on Kamala Markandaya,* Vimal Prakashan, Ghaziabad, 1984.

14. Markandaya, K., *A Silence of Desire,* Sagar Publications, New Delhi, 1968.

15. Chandrasekharan, K.R., *"East and West in the Novels of Kamala Markandaya" in Critical Essays on Indian Writer in English, ed. By M.K. Naik, et.al.,* McMillan, Madras, 1977.

16. Iyenger, K. R. S., *Indian Writing in English,* Sterling, New Delhi, 1983.

17. Williams, H.N., *Indo-Anglian Literature,* Orient Longman, New Delhi, 1976.

18. Prasad, H.M., *Arun Joshi,* Arnold Heinemann, New Delhi, 1985.

5

The Emerging Self Towards Completion

If we go through Forster's **A Passage to India,** we find the disruptive effect of imperial politics on the British residents of India, **Some Inner Fury** depicts with greater tenderness how private personal emotion is muted and individual love ruined by confusing, convulsive, political upheaval. The novel explores the interaction between two individuals belonging to two races, two nations and two cultures with admirable understanding. The novel also brings out the inner strength of Kamala Markandaya's women. Like **Nectar in Sieve** and **Possession, Some Inner Fury** is a first person narrative written in an autobiographical mould. But Mira, the heroine of the novel is different from both Rukmani and Anasuya. Mira is an educated and sophisticated girl and thereby she enjoys greater advantage in comparison with Rukmani. She imbibes the virtues of both cultures. Anasuya is also equipped like her, but she is not the heroine of the novel, nor is she so positive. The novel presents the stream of Mira's consciousness. Her autobiographical narrative flows from an agitated and emotionally surcharged mind:

> I had not been home for a long time, and so I had forgotten the little silver box lying in my cupboard which no one even touched. A beautiful thing of

> filigree, with raised design of lotus flowers which I knew was there though I had to feel for it with my fingertips, it was so worn away. I opened it, and inside was the scrap of material I saw torn from Richard's sleeve, from his upper arm where the flesh was like milk.... The dust was still.... I trembled like a coward standing there.... And then the slow pain came seeping up, filling my throat with grief, flowing from throat to temple. (Markandaya, 1956, 9)

She calls to mind the tale of her life and family with emotional tenderness. She belonged to an educated, moderately forward mofassil family. Kitsmay is a thoroughly westernized son who brings with him British mannerism, Oxford gossip and British acquaintance, Richard Marlowe. The family consists of the reticent father, quietly efficient Amma, the young Mirabai, the silent Govind, the garrulous uncle and the ubiquitous Dodama. They receive Richard with courtesy and good grace. Their house was fully equipped to suit the taste of those used to modern western way of life:

> The house itself was equipped to cope with both Europeans and Indians: there were two dining rooms, two kitchens, even two sets of servants, the one lot knowing Indian cookery and service, the other, trained by European memsahibs, knowing how to deal with such abominations as meet and capable of waiting at table.(Markandaya,1956,29)

The youngest is Mira and therefore the ablest to withstand the heat and strains of outings. She accompanies Richard frequently and gradually she develops intimacy with Richard. The mother dislikes this intimacy but she does not know to express it without being rude. After Richard's departure, the family selects a bride for Kit. Premala is brought to the family to be approved by the members. Premala is a typical Indian girl, shy and conventional by nature. She endeavours to change herself according to the taste of the westernized family. Their marriage is performed with a lot of pomp and show but it reaffirms Premala's personal virtues of simplicity and religiosity. Roshan, one of Kit's westernized friends, leaves a mark on the people by his unconventional but lovable nature. Kit takes up a job, settles down in a state capital and invites Mira to visit her. Richard also visits simultaneously. Mira gets acquainted with Roshan, likes her work and decides to work for her paper. In the process of preparing a report on a peasant resettlement in a neighbourhood, she comes across Richard at the government house. He takes her to the model village and shows her around. Their intimacy grows into love. Kit is a popular and responsible officer and he is frequently at the centre of social activities, but Premala is unable to adjust herself to the world of Kit. Kit suggests that she might find distraction in a visit to village in Mira's company. It is thus Premala comes to get involved in the progress of school building which is the dream of Hickey.

At the same time, the silent, introvert Govind takes to civil disobedience. He turns into a champion of violence and seeks Roshan's support for his activities. When he faces the change of burning the gazette, Roshan rescues him by swearing that he had been in her house in the night of the incident. To give a semblance of reality to this lie, they start living together. Richard who was on an official tour, comes back suddenly with a bout of malaria and six weeks leave. He goes with Mira on a 'honeymoon', part of the way by car and later by any mode of transport that they come across. They go south to the end of land and Kanya Kumari with nothing more than a single suitcase between them, eating and drinking wherever they could, finding simple shelters, making love and enjoying life. They enjoyed their life as a thrilling experience. But the dream is broken by an acid bomb aimed at Richard as he stands at the empty bazaar of the city. He has to face abusive posters warning the foreigners to leave.

With Mira there is a party at the government house where Kit goes as Premala has left for village. During the party, there comes a high gale and power breaks down, and natives rush to the dance hall. Govind is with them demanding to know where Premala is. Learning that she had gone to village, he drags them urgently to the car and they rush to the village in the rains. By the time they reach there, the school building is on fire. Premala is dead in a room of the burning school. Kit turns round on the associates of Govind who had been responsible for fire and abuse them and rushes out towards his car. But a knife is thrown from among the crowd and Kit dies in the hands of Mira. Hickey proclaims that he has seen Govind throw the dagger that killed Kit. Govind is arrested and put on trial. The whole proceedings depend on Hickey's words against Mira's. Mira swears that she had thrown her arms around Govind as Kit left the hut and therefore it is impossible for him to have thrown the dagger. Hickey reiterates that he had seen Govind throw the dagger. Before the issue could be decided the court is mobbed by slogan-shouting crowds and Govind is taken away. Mira also realizes that it is no longer possible for her to keep herself aloof from the people of her own age and maintain her relationship with Richard. And therefore she leaves Richard behind and joins the crowd:

> Go? Leave the man I loved to go with? these people? What did they mean to me, what could they mean, more than the man I loved? They were my people - those others were his. Did it mean something then - all this 'your people' and 'my people' ? Or did it have its being and again its strength from ceaseless repetition? They are nothing to you, cried my heart. Nothing, nothing. If you go now there will be no meaning in anything, ever more. But that stark illuminated movement - of madness? Of sanity? I knew Richard must stay. For us there was no other way, the forces that pulled us apart were too strong. (Markandaya, 1956, 285)

The story brings home several important factors. Different characters stand for different situations, values and attitudes. A detailed analysis of the character and their symbolic dimensions will reveal the central message of the novel. The characters who constitute the dramatis personal of the novel **Some Inner Fury** are Kitsmay, Premala, Govind, Rohan, Richard and Mira. K.R. Chandrashekran goes to the extent of describing **Some Inner Fury** as a war cry against Britain. (Chandra Shekheran,1968,68) Mr. A.V. Krishna Rao comments that:Markandaya dramatizes in this novel not only the political upheaval that wrecks the interracial love of Mira and Richard but also the moral nihilism of the generation of Anglo-Philes of which Kit is the representative. (Krishna Rao,1984,6)Stephen Heinenway remarks, "Markandaya deftly shows that it is British superiority and lack of understanding which provoke the violent reactions for many Indians". (Hemingway,1975,65)

He declares that the novelist fails to wrestle the deeper implications of social situation created by the western impact. There are indeed varying opinions about the implication of the encounter between two races and two cultures. But a careful reading of the novel reveals that Markandaya shows an authentic objective and balanced approach to Indo-British relationship. The novel explores the ambivalence of inter racial relationship, or cultural dualism. Kitsmay is a westernized character abiding the worst that the West has to offer. He is an anglicized Indian, loyal to the western culture and impatient with Indian traditional modes and values represented by Dodamma, Mira, Premala. He is self-centered, self-indulgent, unmindful of hurting others. He can be compared with Sanad Shivpal of Nayantara Sehgal's **A Time to be Happy**, and Krishnan of **The Dark Dancer** by B. Rajan. Sanad Shivpal is the son of a rich man, a product of the public school and an executive in a mercantile firm, facing the problem of regaining his roots, of belonging. It occurs to him that his parents have gone to a great deal of trouble and expense in moulding him to be a figure that will never have a reality. He makes his dilemma clear when he says:

> I don't belong entirely to India. I can't. My education, my upbringing and my sense of values have all

> combined to make me un-Indian, what do I have in common with me most of my country men? (Sehgal, 1973,147)

In the novel **The Dark Dancer**, Krishnan comes back from Cambridge to India which has an indifferent sky for him. His sense of alienation is apparent from the beginning. But in spite of his constant hairsplitting analysis of the unreasonable demands of society he submits to every family decision. He wants to belong but his marriage is ruined by his wavering between Cynthis and Kamala. He himself analyses the difference between them:

> She (Cynthis) came from a tradition which included non-conformity and dissent amongst attributes.... His on the contrary was a background completely conformist where the map of one's life was drawn even before one's first cry (Rajan,1959,165)

Krishnan suddenly discovers the basic difference between them and finds the right path. Kitsmay is like Krishnan and Sanad Shivpal in his western orientation, but his westernization is deeper than theirs. Meenakshi Mukherjee rightly remarks that, "Kit is entirely a product of the west and emerges as a stereotyped **Burra Sahib**". (Mukherjee, 1971, 83) He is impatient with Premala for her insufficiencies even during their courtship but he marries her. They are never able to make a harmony between them and therefore Premala divorced herself by her social service activities. In fact, the lack of perfect harmony in domestic orbit throws her out to the bigger world of public works. There is, however, something pressing forth from the unconscious of Kitsmay. He is fully westernized but he treats his wife in the manner in which a typical Indian husband does. He lacks that considerateness which thoroughly westernized Indian may be expected to show. In his character there is no conscious desire for belonging to the soil as we find in Sanad or Krishnan. In him the influence of the West is not skin-deep; it is in his mental make up. Consequently he fails to emerge as a real, living, round character in the milieu of Indian society of which he is a part. He is a symbol of the inflictions of the West and since he has thrown his roots into the alien rocks, he remains an outsider, a fringe character in the novel.

The sweetest and most clearly Indian character in the novel is Premala . Prof Iyenger describes her as the most heroic character of the novel. Meenakshi Mukherjee is of the opinion that "she is idealized to the extent of being unreal". ((Mukherjee, 1971, 83). In truth, Premala is a home-spun, devout Hindu, innocent, modest and unpretentious, universally loved for her sweetness and charm. She finds no place in the westernized world of Kit. As a result she grows lonely and satisfies her motherhood by possessing an orphan girl. But this orphan is not able to quench her desires. Kitsmay is sensitive to the yearnings of the women in her. Govind could sense this even before the marriage and Premala is fully aware of Govind's pattern of thinking. But she cannot take a lover, nor would Govind ever approve of it. She sublimates her feelings in her school work. At a time when Kit and Premala have grown far apart, she is asphyxiated - the innocent victim of a political act, the burning of the village school, and Kitsmay is tabbed in the aftermath. Both are invested with symbolic qualities. Premala is silent but strong "Mother Indian"(Iyenger,1973,332) Kit on the other hand is, "the complacent, well placed, upholder of the old order, the crutch on which British India leaned too heavily".(Hemingway,1975,62)

She is a representative Indian woman, a recurring character in Indo-English novel. She is like Kamala in **The Dark Dancer** and Laila in **Sunlight on a Broken Column** showing the qualities of mysterious strength, sense of sacrifice, a brief in non-violence exuding the smell of the soil. In the failure of relationship between Kit and Premala we may discern the refusal of basic Indian values to be dominated by westernization. Kitsmay is a symbol of the superficiality, slavish mentality and lack of oneness with one's own country. In other words, he crystallizes the shabby features of the Western culture. Premala on the other hand, symbolizes the virtues of Indian life and culture. It is obvious that the worst of the western culture cannot be absorbed in the fabric of Indian life.

The next important character is Govind who contributes to the development of the story and opens up a new dimension of racial relationship. Right from the beginning he is outlined in sinister colours. He is silent, forbidding and converses in mono-syllables. He disapproves Kit's westernized traits. He is fanatic in his love for his country and holds everything in contempt which is alien from his point of view. Mira describes his attitude to the western influence on India in most clear terms:

> Govind was not and had never been a part of it. To him it was the product of a culture which was not his own – the culture of an aloof and alien race twisted in the process of transplantation from its whole-and, and so divorced from the people of the country as to be no longer real. Or those who participated in it he had a savage harsh contempt. (Markandaya,1955,129)

Govind "seems doomed to be the recipient of God's disfavour". ".(Hemingway,1975,62) He not only detests Kit for personal and political reasons, he also dislikes the well meaning English missionary:

> To him missionaries were not merely men who assaulted the religion which was his though he might not cherish it impugning its austere dignities in a hundred ways; they were also white men, who not only set up their alien and unwanted institutions in the land but who, for the preservation of these institutions sided the country, and with whom otherwise they had little in common. (Markandaya, 1955, 142)

In Govind we find the politics of violence and non-violence who stands as an apostle and he resorts to every possible device to free his country from the clutches of the

British rulers. Ultimately he is arrested for Kit's murder and faces a partial and inconclusive trial reminiscent of Aziz's experience in **A Passage to India**. Mira, torn between loyalties to the dead Kit and the living Govind points out an ethnic truth: "Govind belonged to his country and Kitsmay didn't".(Markandaya,1955,247)

He is the symbol of hostility to British an western culture. The hatred against the alien rule finds and expression through his violent acts against them and his dislike of the western culture is vindicated by his reaction to the character of Kitsmay and deep understanding for Premala. His silent love for Premala is an indirect vindication of his clinging to the essential spirit of Indian culture. In his character Kamala Markandaya creates a representative of a large section of Indians who held radical opposition to both British rule and alien culture.

Another fascinating representation of Quit India campaign is Roshan . As a contrast to Premala she is a sophisticated woman with glaring stubbornness and a remarkable degree of sensibility. Unlike Premala she represents the virile and the assertive side of the feminine. She is a liberated modern woman of India, having been educated in England and brought on western values, she is, in fact, a product of dual centered both and moved in both with ease and nonchalance"[17](Markandaya,1955,121) Though she has assimilated western culture and education, yet she has a truly Indian heart. She takes willing participation in political struggle against Britain. When he is released after serving a term of imprisonment and Mira asks her if she was sorry for having served a sentence, she gives a bold reply:

> What do you think? Of course I'm not sorry. I'd rather go to the devil my own way than be led to heaven by anyone else. And I wouldn't give up being free like that for anything it hasn't always been that way - no, not even for me. (Markandaya,1955,16)

Roshan resembles Rajeshwari in the novel **Kandan, the Patriot,** for both of them are symbols of resurgence of Indian women in the wake of national movement. Roshan helps Govind and plays big sister and provides a liberating influence throughout the novel. She serves as the hovering angel at the eleventh hour as she directs the mob and frees Govind from the British Court. In Roshan we find the reality of cultural coexistence, the truth of ambivalence, neither rejecting a culture fully nor accepting another in totality. The attempt is to accept both with understanding and reason. This facet of reality finds its best expression in the relationship between Richard and Mira. The relationship between Richard and Mira is the nucleus of the novel and the central key to Markandaya's exploration into racial relationship. Richard is an unconventional Englishman endowed with sweetness and light of western enlightenment. Chandrashekhran rightly remarks that he presents Kamala Markandaya's "warm appreciation of the Englishman as an individual". (Chadrashekharan, 1968, 339)

He is not a typical representative of British Raj in India; to the contrary he is remarkably sensitive and sensible. Almost throughout the novel he stands as a contrast to the character of Kitamay. He is always willing to adapt himself to the alien environment without discarding his own rich sensibility. Through his one month's stay he endears himself to all the member of Kit's family. He is a perfect gentleman and an ideal lover. He is cautious to the point of visiting Mira's home to seek her mother's consent for their marriage. Mira is his emotional counterpart. The relationship between Richard and Mira is an ideal possibility of cultural coexistence. Mira is the central consciousness of the novel, the most roundly presented character with sensitivity and imaginative vigour. She is brought up in a westernized household where they have two dining halls and two sets of cooks, where the members frequently visit clubs and participate in dance and song. She is an educated modernized conscious Indian woman who can afford to honour personal relationship unhurt by racial differences. When they are enjoying their life in the honeymoon part of the novel, in the bazaar, a bomb is thrown on Richard and anti-British slogans and posters are shown everywhere; Richard is disturbed. She tries to convince him:

> Richard.... you mustn't think.... this feeling isn't for you. Or - or for people like you.... You must believe me, I would not lie to you. Listen to me, I've told you.... This feeling isn't for you. Do you think I don't know? (Markandaya,1955,217-8)

Richard asks: "Do you really think people can be singled out like that? One by one, each as an individual? At a time like this? - After two days?" (Markandaya,1955,218)

Yes, the situation grows more critical and sprawling, and the time comes when Mira can hold no longer. She has to make a choice between joining the procession of Indian patriots and staying away from it with Richard, she realizes that they cannot stay together.

> When the tail of the procession went through the door, I would join it, and Richard would stay behind. This was not a time for decision, for he knew he could not come with me, and I knew I could not stay: it was simply the time for parting. (Markandaya,1955,285)

The people in the procession may not have any individual reality for her, but she cannot resist the pull of the procession because it has got the sanction of racial and national consciousness. She reflects:

> They were my people - those other were him. Did it mean something then all this 'your people' and 'my people'? Or did it have its being and again its strength from ceaseless repetition? They are nothing to you, cried my heart. Nothing, nothing. If you go now there will be no meaning in anything, ever more. But that stark illuminated movement - of madness? Of sanity? - Want, and I knew I would go, even as I knew Richard must stay. For us there was no other way, the forces that pulled us apart were too strong. (Markandaya, 1955, 285)

This passage is reminiscent of the famous last line of **A Passage to India**. It appears that the novel ends on a note of disunion, but the truth is that it concludes with an intense awareness of love, tenderness and understanding. Its real meaning can be brought to focus if it is compared with Manohar Malgonkar's **Combat of Shadows,** Raja Rao's **The Serpent and the Rope** and Anita Desai's **Bye-Bye Blackbird** because all these novels cut across various crusts of human relationship against the backdrop of ethnic encounter. In all these novels, the central motive is to explore the dilemma of personal relationship and racial prejudice in terms of sex, love and marriage. **Combat of Shadows** is a story of Henry Winton, a British planatation manager and Ruby Miranda, a beautiful Anglo-Indian girl whom he appoints as a school teacher to break the loneliness and monotony of planter's life in the remote corner of North-Eastern Assam. Ruby feels unwanted and rootless in India and thus tries to become Henry's wife with a view to escaping from the brown world and entering into the world of the white. Henry Winton finds in Eddie Trevor an Eurasian rival which she cannot bear with. He goes to England for vacation and comes back married. Stung by the disloyalty of Winton. Ruby swears to take revenge. She gets a suitable chance when jean, Henry's wife falls in love with Eddi and decides to marry him. Before the marriage could take place, Eddi gets killed by an elephant and Jean goes away. Thoroughly experienced, Henry Winton now gets genuinely interested in Ruby and would like to marry her. But Ruby has a different plan and she gets Henry killed in the fire with the help of the village man. The relationship between Ruby and Winton is radically different from that of Richard Marlowe and Mira. To Henry, Ruby is,

> .... the rare mixture of the submissiveness and the surrender of oriental womanhood with the freedom an gaiety of the West and of course the breathtaking figure and good looks and colouring which had been a gift of both the West and the East. She was not

> the kind of woman who analyzed your short-comings; Ruby Miranda was content with him the way he was, even prepared to sacrifice the love of her childhood sweetheart for him. (Malgonker,1968,116)

Behind the attitude of Henry Winton we find a cluster of attitudes working from the inside of his mind. Since he belongs to the European race he nourishes a sense of superiority and in spite of his protest against Jean's admission that he did not marry Ruby, because of the sense of racial superiority, he cannot be said to be free from racial pride. Ruby also accepts the job of a teacher on Henry's plantation with the intention of winning and marrying the white man who is a passport to the dream world of Eurasian womanhood. Like most of her fellow Anglo-Indians, Ruby is unhappy with her Indian connection and she wants to make herself complete by marrying a Whiteman. In her, Manohar Malgonker finds the dim contours of the dream of Anglo-India:

> She could never have explained to Henry Winton the throbbing compulsive craving of Anglo-India to seek living kinship with the West; the desperate, daily struggle of separation and alignment, the tight clutching of the tenuous, often imaginary strands of relationships with the sahibs, the constant vigilance against further assimilation with the smothering, enveloping people of the Indian soil. . (Malgonker, 1968, 103)

Contrary to her expectations, Ruby finds, only a lust for the flesh in the relationship with Henry Winton. In the next part of the novel when Henry is humbled by slow discovery of his wife's disloyalty, he is able to love Ruby. Humbled and chastened by his tragic experience of a lusterless and loveless married life, he turns to Ruby without fear, pride and racial prejudice. But it was too late and Ruby has plunged herself into irreversible frustration and lack of faith. She becomes a symbol of general Anglo-Indian belief that there is nothing but sorrow and disappointment in their seeking kinship with the White Race. She is blind by racial hatred and refuses to notice the change that has dawned upon Henry Winton. In Kamala Markandaya the situation is altogether different. The relationship between Richard and Mira is based upon mutual attraction, understanding and it is also a communion of deeper level of souls. Racial and cultural differences do not interfere in their positive relationship. In their physical union there is always poetry, love and rare tenderness. On the other hand, Ruby and Henry work at cross purposes and they indulge in casual sex. Lust not love prompts their relationship. Passions of fear, suspicion, pride, desire and aversion aroused by racial and cultural prejudice scuttle their enduring relationship. In fact, Markandaya and Malgonkar have approached the subject of interracial and intercultural relationship in two different ways. They stand on two extreme points of possibilities with regard to this subject. But they come to the same conclusion that there is much disappointment and suffering for the people who try to break racial and cultural barriers and come together. However, it is relevant to observe that both the novels were written just before independence. Naturally, the time was not ripe for the conceptualizations of such relationships. The circumstances of history and changing equations on the political chess-board make little difference in genuine personal relationship. In a relationship of love the separate identities mingle and merge and yet these remain inviolate and intact. Though at times the choice can be agonizing. Mira does not suffer from any conflict of identities, her love for India. The underlying suggestion is that both patriotism and man-woman love are expressions of love. Despite the burning Kernel of agony there is lucidity about Mira's thinking. The conflict is on the surface. Deep within their love remains unchanging through history compels them to take different positions. The processions exercises a magnetic pull on Mira. She knows that her not joining it would be as impossible as Richard joining it. But they regard each other with deep understanding. Hence there is no wrench of betrayal, no romantic yearning for the impossible. Mira is not a type-character, not a patriot who sacrifices her personal love. Her love for Richard is too precious to be sacrificed. But at the same time she cannot ignore the suffering and humiliation of the whole nation under for domination. She belongs to these people and their suffering she feels in her own blood and soul. in Mira who merges her own lot with the lot of her people there is an inner conflict but no contradiction. Women in Kamala Markandaya'a world are long suffering strongcreatures. They act not from random impulse but from strong conviction.

At the time, when a nation is engaged in a painful struggle for liberation it is but natural that the conflict of loyalties is experienced by some individuals. Markandaya shows the impact this powerful conflict on the family of Kit who is himself loyal to the British government. But his cousin, Govind who is bent upon making the supreme of his own life for freeing his country from Whitman's domination. Mira is in love with an Englishman and she has experienced the kind of deep harmony and mutuality in love to which considerations of nationality and race can make no difference. There is violence in the air. Govind and his men are not content with destroying property and dislocation the rule of law; they are bent upon drawing blood. The burning of the school building is a heart-breaking incident. It assumes terrible overtones when Premala is discovered to have been killed in the fire. Premala is one of the most lovable characters. Her husband, the westernized Kit is also stabbed to death. When the great storms of history blow the little lives of the individuals are tossed about like tiny boats. Nevertheless, each individual leaves behind his imprint. Everything depends on the way he braves the storm. There are 'codes' or principle to which some men of character hold fast while the others choose to drift about like driftwood. Mira is not a sentimental creature. She understands the effect of the inexorable forces of history, and realizes with perfect calm that individual occupy an insignificant place in the scheme of things. When the time comes for the parting of way, Richard automatically joins the group of Englishmen, Mira with the same kind of inevitability joins her countrymen. Mira says, "For us there was no other way, the forces that pulled us apart were too strong".(Markandaya,1955,174) In a great upheaval of history, a few individuals may get hurt or even eliminated. There is nothing unusual or depressing about it, though it spells tragedy and disaster to the individual:

> But what matters to the universe. I said to myself, if now and then a world is born or a star should die; or what matter to the world if here and there a man should fall or a head or a heart should break. (Markandaya, 1955, 192)

Mira is sweet and soft and has also the hardness of granite in her character. She rationalizes in an impersonal tone though her own heart is broken and her own world is about to die like a star. Kamala Markandaya does not always invest her suffering female characters with an aura of dignity. Often her women seem to be burnt-out cases – fragile creatures battered by life. A fatalistic attitude to life and a philosophy of passive suffering are indicated by Markandaya as typical of India, especially of her women. The major characters in **Nectar in a Sieve** bear "the slings and arrows of fortune" most passively the passive and uncomplaining suffering of Granny is heart-breaking. She ekes out a miserable existence sitting all day in the street selling a few annas' worth of nuts and vegetables. When Rukmani expresses her fear of such a life Granny tells her: "It is not unbearable. One gets used to it". Rukmani while discussing her lot with the missionary, Kenny remarks,

> What is our companion from birth to death, familiar as the seasons on the earth, varying only in degree. What profits to bewail that which has always been and cannot change. (Markandaya, 1955, 113)

We can assume that India is a country where fatalism is the prevailing creed, yet there is little room for initiative or enterprise. Sarojini, the heroine of **A Silence of Desire** is suffering from a painful tumour but she refuses to go to a hospital for treatment. This is partly because according to her scale of values the body does not come first in the list of priorities. Instead of seeking medical treatment she regularly worships the "tulasi" plant in her courtyard and for the cure of her affliction she goes to the Swamy. To Sarojini Swamy who doctors the soul is the real healer rather than the doctor who treats only the body. Kamala Markandaya looks at the holymen - the Swamis of India through the eyes of her devout and believing women characters. **In Possession** and **A Silence of Desire** has the Swamy in the centre of quiet strength. He discovers Val and guides him to destiny. To Swamy Caroline is not a positive influence on Val but she is necessary Val cannot grow without experience. From the Swamy's point of view Caroline is a stage in Val's schooling. Even as the Swamy permit Val to leave for England he is confident that he will ultimately return to him. After Val is comfortably established in London, he finds that he cannot do any painting because the fountain of inspiration has dried up within him. Caroline keeps him going from day to day by producing the forged letters supposed to have been written by Swamy. Disillusionment and disappointment at last drive Val back to India. The tug-of-war between Swamy and Caroline for the control of Val is symbolic. It is a clash between two sets of values - western materialism an Indian spiritualism. Caroline returns to India to take possession of Val, and complains that he has returned to a mere wilderness. To this the Swamy replies, "Even this wasteland may have something to show other than what you have seen". (Markandaya, 1960, 119)

In Swamy's statement there is the suggestion that the waste land that is India can be redeemed and her soul saved, only by a return to her ancient spiritual ways. Capitulation to the charms of the West and imitation of her one fundamentally different ways which can result only in the degradation and decay of her soul. The Swamy thus becomes a dominant figure in the novel. Caroline who belongs to the West and Lalitha in **Two Virgins** who is lured by the false glitter of the west do not find favor with Kamala Markandaya. They lack the quiet faith of the typical Indian women who refuse to bow down before misery and misfortune. They also refuse to be swayed by the kind of artificiality that lures Lalitha to her doom. The typical Indian woman is like this great land itself. Ravaged by the floods and droughts of misery, bound to ancient customs - to the temples, Swamys and rhythm of nature, they are patient and submissive. One is reminded of Jayamma and Kamala and Rukmani who submit and suffer. One is also reminded of Mira who can rise to the occasion and take very crucial decisions. Some women like Kunthi in **Nectar in a Sieve** are deviants and some like Ira in the same compelled by circumstances to deviate from the proper path.

For Kamala Markandaya woman is a sufferer. Like Rukmani she is a mother of sorrows. And it is not only Rukmani but almost all women characters in the novels of Kamala Markandaya may be described as victims. Often they remind us of women in Hardy's fiction who are always dogged by misfortune. In Hardy man is a plaything at the hands of time of chance of destiny. In Kamala Markandaya the socio-economic factors and the ancient mode of life in this long suffering land are at the root of women's suffering. Even the "modern" women of Kamala Markandaya are passive. They lack initiative and the power of defiance. Commenting on the major themes of the Indo-Anglian novel K.B.Vaid says that among the major thematic preoccupations of the Indo-Anglian novelists are, "portrayal of poverty, hunger and disease: portrayal of widespread social evils and tensions; examination of the survivals of the past; explorations of the hybrid culture, of the dislocations and conflicts in a tradition-ridden society under the impact of an incipient, half-hearted industrialization:. To these one may add the themes of conflict between tradition and modernity, of man's loneliness and rootlessness. Women who play a very important part in India's mythology and culture and system of values emerge as major characters often demonstrating the drift of Indian society. Kamala Markandaya projects her women characters as representatives of the Indian mode of living and thinking. It has become a library stereotype to identify these woman with the Indian earth – with Mother India.

The author shows her women grappling with problems which transcend a mere economic or social definition. They are engaged in battles of different types at the different fronts of life. Not all of them are domestic like Kamala in **A Handful of Rice** of Rukmani **Nectar in a Sieve. Some Inner Fury** also has a women narrator, Mira, the heroine, but she is entirely different from Rukmani, the woman narrator of her first novel Mira is sophisticated and westernized, and the central theme of the novel may be said to be the clash between passion and patriotism and the inner fury of passion is symbolic of the Indian passion for independence. The background is urban and much vaster than that of her first novel and the characters more varied.

In the novel, the story begins with the return of Mira's brother Kiti with his Oxford friend Richard, Govind, her adopted brother, Premala, who marries Kit, and Roshan, the rich lady who fishes in the troubled waters o emancipation and revolutionary politics, are the principal dramatis personal. There is, besides, Hickey, the missionary, a variation of Kenny of **Nectar in a Sieve**. Almost as in a typical Hardy novel, intensified clash and malignant forces are let loose. Govind wishing to escape from his hopeless love for Premala, becomes a revolutionary; Premala escaping from the stifling atmosphere of her husband's home as often as she can, helps Hickey in his humanitarian work' and Mira and Richard seek happiness in each other's arms. But the Quit India Movement overtakes them, and carries them along and finally engulfs them. It is a ghastly mistake certainly, but revolutions breed such mistakes; Premala dies of suffocation; Kit dies of knife-wound, and Richard falls a victim to mob fury. Mira returns to her home, to be shut with the ghosts of her memories; and from time to time the slow pain comes" seeping up, filling up my throat with grief, flowing from throat to temple". It is a tragedy engineered by politics; and in both (**Nectar in a Sieve** and **Some Inner Fury**) novels the chief characters transcend the bludgeoning of economic or political mischance and assert the unconquerable spirit of humanity.

Yes, it is a love story which takes place against the background of the freedom movement of India. It appears in the final analysis that this socio-political novel of modern India is symbolically significant on two levels: first it is about the emotional inner fury of Mira; secondly, it is about the wider inner fury of a resurgent nation. Mira regards her personal passion-her own emotional upheaval-as secondary to the great convulsion of history involving the destiny of a nation. Clearly Mira knows the distinction between lust and love. The former is personal, and the latter, impersonal; the former is an appetite hungering for appeasement, and the latter the will to make the supreme sacrifice. This is how it all goes.

All the works of Kamala Markandaya illustrate her deep sense of multiculturality that, of course, leads to ambivalence of multiculturality, replete with diasporic dilemmas and the emergence of the self as subaltern.

REFERENCES

1. Markandaya, K., *Some Inner Fury*, New York, John Dey, 1956.
2. Chandra Shekheran, K.R., *"East and West, the Novel of Kamala Markandaya"*, in *Critical Essays on Indian Writing in English,* (ed.) M.K. Naik, et.al. Dharwar, Karnatake University Press, 1968
3. Krishna Rao, A.V., *"Continuity and Change in the Novel of Kamala Markandaya"*, in *Perspectives on Kamala Markandaya,* (ed) Dr. M. Prasad, Vimal Prakashan, Ghaziabad, 1984.
4. Heimenway, S., *The Novel of India,* Writer Workshop, 1975.
5. Sehgal, N., *A Time To Be Happy,* Jaico Publications, Bombay, 1973.
6. Rajan, B., The Dark Dancer, Heinemann, London, 1959.
7. Mukherjee, M., *Twice Born Fiction,* Arnold Heinemann, New Delhi, 1971.

8. Iyenger, K..R..S., *Indian Writing in English,* Asia Publishing House, Bombay, 1973.

9. Markandaya, K., *Some Inner Fury,* Putnam & Co., London, 1955.

10. Malgonkar, M., *Combat of Shadows,* Hind Pocket Books, Delhi, 1968.

Bibliography

A. Primary Sources

Marandays, Kamala : Nectar in a Sieve, Jaico Publishing House, Bombay 1955.

——: Some Inner Fury, Putnam & Co., London, 1955.

——: A Silence of Desire, Four Square Books, London, 1960.

——: Possession, Jaico Publishing, House, Bombay, 1963.

——: A Hand Full of Rice, Orient Paperbacks, New Delhi, 1966.

——: The Coffer Dams, Hind Pocket Books (n.d.), Delhi.

——: The Nowhere Man, Orient Longman, Bombay, 1975.

——: Two Virgins, Vikas Publishing House, New Delhi, 1977.

——: The Golden Honeycomb, B.I. Publications, New Delhi, 1977.

——: Pleasure City, Chatto and Windus, London, 1982.

B. Secondary Sources

Achebe, Chinua : Things Fall Apart, Heinemannn, London, 1958.

——: No Longer at Ease, Heinemann African Writer Series, London.

Amirthanayagam, Guy: Writers in East-West Encounter, The McMillan Press Ltd.,

London, 1882.

Austen, Jane : Poets and Story-tellers, Constable, London, 1960.

Bakhtiyar, Iqbal: The Novel in Modern India, P.E.N. All India Centre, Bombay, 1984.

Carroll, David: Arrow of God, Longman York Press, London, 1980.

Clark, T.W.: The Novel in India, George Allen & Unwin, London, 1970.

Derret, M.E. : The Modern Indian Novel in English: A Comparative Approach, Universe Libre De Bruxelles, 1966.

Desai, Anita : Bye-Bye Blackbird, Hind Pocket Books, Delhi, 1971.

Dutton, G.: The Literature of Australia, Penguin Books, Adelaide, 1964.

Ellison, Ralph: Inevitable Man, The New American Library, New York,1960.

Ewers, J.K.: Creative Writing in Australia, Georgian House, Melbourne, 1945.

Forster, E.M.: A Passage to India, Penguin Books, Harmondsworth, 1941.

Green, H.M : A History of Australian Literature, Pure and Applied, Angus and Robertson, Sydney,1962.

Harrex, S.C. : The Fire and the Offering: The English Language Novel of India (1935-70), 2 Volumes, Writers Workshop, Calcutta, 1977 and 1978.

Hemengway, Stephen: The Novel of India (Vol.2:Indo-Anglian Novel), Ignaitips Writers Workshop, Calcutta, 1975.

Iyengar, K.R. Srinivasa: Indian Writing in English, Asia Publishing House, Bombay, 1973.

——: Two Cheers for the Commonwealth, Asia Publishing House, Bombay, 1970.

Jones, E.D. : African Literature Today, Heinemann Educational Books Ltd., London, 1981.

——: African Literature Today, No.5, The Novel in Africa, Heinemann Educational Books Ltd. London, 1982.

Joseph, Margaret P. : Kamala Markandaya, Arnold Heinemann, New Delhi, 1980.

Joshi, Arun : The Last Labyrinth, Orient Paperback, New Delhi, 1981.

Jussawalla, Adil: New Writing From India, Penguin Maryland, 1974.

Kalinnikova, Klena J.: Indian-English Literature: A Survey, Vimal Prakashan, Ghaziabad, 1982.

Kurtz, Paul : The Fullness of Life, Horizon Press, New York, 1974.

Lubbock, Percy : The Craft of Fiction, B.I. Publications, Madras, 1979.

Malgonkar, Manohar: Combat of Shadows, Hamish Hamilton, London, 1962.

Mc Cutchion, David : Indian Writing in English, Writers Workshop, Calcutta, 1969.

Mehta, P.P. : Indo-Anglian Fiction, Prakash Book Depot, Bareilly, 1979.

Michael, Gilkes : Wilson Harris and the Caribbean Novel, Longman, 1975.

Moore, T.I. : Social Patterns in Australian Literature, University of California Press, Berkeley, 1971.

Mukherjee, Meenakshi: The Twice-Born Fiction: Themes and Techniques of the Indian Novel in English, Arnold-Heinemann, New Delhi, 1971.

——: Considerations, Allied Publishers Private Ltd., New Delhi, 1977.

Murti, K V Suryanarayan : Kohinoor in the Crown: Critical Study in Indian English Literature.

Naik, M.K. : Critical Essays on Indian Writing in English, the McMillan Company of India, Madrass, 1977.

——: Aspects of Indian Writing in English, The Macmillan Company of India, Madrass, 1979.

Naipal, V.S. : The Middle Passage, Penguin, Harmondsworth, 1969.

Narasimhaiah, C.D : Fiction and the Reading Public in India, University of Mysore, 1967.

——: The Swan and the Eagle, Indian Institute of Advanced Study, Simla, 1969.

——: Indian Literature of the Past Fifty Years 1917-1967, University of Mysore, 1970.

——: Awakened Conscience, Sterling Publisher Pvt., Ltd., New Delhi, 1978.

——: Commonwealth Literature, Oxford University Press, New Delhi, 1976.

Narayan, R.K. : Next Sunday, Orient Paperbacks, New Delhi, 1965.

Narsimah, Raja : Sensibility Under Stress: Aspects of Indo-English Fiction, Ashajanak Prakashan, New Delhi, 1976.

Nicholson, Kai : Social Problems in the Indo-Anglian and the Anglo-Indian Novels, Jaico Publishing House, Bombay, 1972.

Parmeswaran, Uma : A Study of Represntative Indo-English Novelists, Vikas Publishing House, New Delhi, 1976.

Phonex, : The Post Thomas Papers of D.H. Lawrence, William Heinemann, London, 1961.

Poddera, A. : Indian Literature, Indian Institute of Advanced Study, Simla, 1972.

Prasad, H.M. : Response: Recent Revelations of Indian Fiction in English, Prakash Book Depot, Barreily, 1983.

——: Arun Joshi, Arnold Heinemann, New Delhi, 1985.

Prasad, Madhusudan : Indian English Novelists: An Anthology of Critical Essay, Sterling Punishers Pvt. Ltd., New Delhi, 1982.

——: Perspectives on Kamala Markandaya, Vimal Prakashan, Ghaziabad, 1984.

Press, John: Commonwealth Literature: Unity and Diversity in a Common Culture, Heinemann, London, 1965.

Raizada, Harish: The Lotus and the Rose: Indian Fiction in English (1850-1947), Faculty of Arts, Aligarh Muslim University, Aligarh, 1978.

Rajan, Balchandra : The Dark Dancer, Heinemann, London, 1959.

Ram. Atma ed.: Perspectives on R.K. Narayan, Vimal Prakashan, Ghaziabad, 1984.

Rao, A.V. Krishna: The Indo-Anglian Novel and the Changing Tradition, Rao & Raghavan, Mysore, 1972.

Rao, Raja: The Serpent and the Rope, John Murrey, London, 1960.

——: Kanthapura, New Directions, New York, 1963.

Rau, Santha Rama : Remember the House, Victor Gollancz, London, 1956.

Sahgal, Nayantara: A Time to Be Happy, Jaico Publication, Bombay, 1952.

Sarma, G.P.: Nationalism in Indo-Anglian Fiction, Sterling Publishers Private Ltd., New Delhi, 1978.

Sharma, K.K. : Indo-English Literature: A Collection of Critical Essays, Vimal Prakashan, Ghaziabad, 1977.

Shirwadkar, Meena : Image of Woman in the Indo-Anglian Novel, Sterling Publishers Pvt. Ltd., New Delhi, 1979.

Singh, R.S : Indian Novel in English, Arnold Heinemann, New Delhi, 1977.

Sinha, Krishna Nadan: Indian Writing in English, Heritage Publishers, New Delhi, 1979.

Spencer, Dorothy M. : Indian Fiction in English, University of Pennsylvania Press, Philadelphia, 1960.

Srivastava, A.K. : Alein Voice, Print House, Lucknow, 1981.

Steiner, George : Extratarritorial, Penguin Books, Harmondsworth, 1969.

Rao, Raja : The Serpent and the Rope, John Murry, London, 1960.

——: Kanthapura, New Directortions, New York, 1963.

Rau, Santha Rama : Remember the House, Victor Gollancz, London, 1956.

Sehgal, Nayantara : A Time To Be Happy, Jaico Publication, Bombay, 1952.

Sarma, G.P. : National in Indo-Anglian Fiction, Sterling Publishers Private Ltd., New Delhi, 1978.

Sharma, K.K. : Indo-English Literature : A Collection of Critical Essays, Vimal Prakashan, Ghaziabad, 1977.

Shirwadmkar, Heena : Image of Woman in the Indo-Anglian Novel, Sterling Publishers Pvt. Ltd., New Delhi, 1979.

Singh, R.S. : Indian Novel in English, Arnold Heinemann, New Delhi, 1977.

Sinha, Krishna Nandan: Indian Writing in English, Heritage Publishers, New Delhi, 1979.

Spencer, Dorothy M. : Indian Fiction in English, University of Pennsylvania Press, Philadelphia, 1960.

Srivastava, A.K. : Alien Voice, Print House, Lucknow, 1981.

Steiner, George : Extraterritorial, Penguin Books, Harmondsworth, 1969.

Trilling, Lionel : Sincerity and Authenticity, Oxford University Press, London, 1972.

Verghese, C.Paul : Problems of the Indian Creative Writing in English, Somaiya Publications, Bombay, 1971.

——: Essays on Indian Writing in English, N.V. Publications, Bombay, 1975.

Walsh, William : A Human Idiom: Literature and Humanity, Chatto and Windus, London, 1970.

—— : A Manifold Voice, Chatto and Windus, London, 1970.

——: Readings in Commonwealth Literature, Clarendon Press, Oxford, 1973.

Wallace, Irving : The Fabulous Originals, Four Square Books, London, 1967.

William, H.M. : Studies in Modern Indian Fiction in English. Writers Workshop, Calcutta, 1973.

——: Indo-Anglian Literature 1800-1970, A Survey, Orient Longman, Madras, 1976.

Journals

Achebe, Chinue : "The Black Writer's Burden" Presence Africaine, 59, 1966, pp.131-39.

—— : "Named for Victoria, Queen of England", New Letters, XI, 1973.

Appasamy, S.P. : "The Golden HoneyComb: A Saga of Princely India by Kamala Markandaya". The Journal of Indian Writing in English, Vol. 6, No. 2, July, 1978.

Chanddha, Mrs. Ramesh: "Heat and Dust and The Coffer Dams A Comparative Study", The Journal of Indian Writing in English, Vol.10, No.182, January-July, 1982.

Chauhan, P.S.: "Kamala Markandaya: Sense and Sensibility", The Literary Criterion, Vol.XII, Nos. 2-3, 1976.

Dunn, T.A.: "Intensity and Cripeness", Journal of Commonwealth Literatuer. No.5, July, 1968.

Fzekiel, Wissim: Puppet Show: Review of Kamala

Markandaya's Two Virgins" The Illustrated Weekly of India, June 15, 1975.

Geethan P. : "Kamala Markandaya: An Interpretation", Commonwealth Quarterly, Vol. 3, No.9. December, 1978.

Gondal, Yogesh Chandra: "Relationship and Dams", Journal of Commonwealth Literature, Vol.VIII, No. 1, June, 1973.

Guruprasad, Thakur : "And Never the Twain Shall Meet: Kamala Markandaya's The Nowhere Men", Language Forum, Vol.VII, Nos. 1-4, April, 1981-March, 1982.

Harrex, S.C. : " A Sense of Identity: The Novels of Kamala Markandaya", Journal of Commonwealth Literature, No.1, June, 1971.

Katamba, V.D. : " The Coffer Dams: An Apology for Techno-Industrialization of Rural India", Vortex 1, October, 1979.

Kumar, Shiv K. : "Tradition and Change in the Novels of Kamala Markandaya", Osmania Journal of English Studies, Vol. VII, No.1, 1969.

Nandkumar, Prema : "Indian Writing in English: Three Cheers", Indian Literature, 13, No.4.

Parmeswaran, Uma : "India for the Western Readers, A Study of Kamala Markandaya's Novels", Texax Quarterly, Vol. X, No. 2, Summer, 1968.

Payne, Robert : "The Homesick Shepherd", Saturday Review, May 23, 1963.

Prasad, Hari Mohan :"The Quintessence of Kamala Markandaya's Art", Commonwealth Quarterly, Vol.3. No.9, December,1978.

Rao, K.S. Narayana : "Kamala Markandaya As Craftsman", Indian Writing Today, 8, April-June, 1969.

——: "Some Notes on the Plots of Kamala Markandaya's Novel", Indian Literature, Vol.XII, No.1, March, 1970.

Rao, Vimale : "Indian Expatriates" Journal of Commonwealth Literature", Vol.X, No.3, April, 1976.

Redfield, Linton & Herskovits : "Memorandum on the Study of Acculturation". American Anthropologist, 1936.

Rosenberg, Jeroneh: "Narative Perspective and Cultural Hisory in Robbery Under Arms", Australian Literary Studies, 6, 1973.

Srivastava, Ramesh K. : "Symbolism in Nectar in a Sieve", Indian Scholar, Vol. I, No. 2, July, 1979.

——: "The Pattern of Hope and Pear in Markandaya's Nectar in a Sieve", The Indian Journal of English Studies, Vol.XX, New Series Vol.1, 1980.

——: "The Theme of Hunger in Bhattacharya and Markandaya", Language Forum, Vol. VII, Nos. 1-4, April 1981, March 1982.

Venkateswaran, Shyamala : "The Language of Kamala Markandaya's Novel", The Literary Criterion, Vol. IX, No.3, Winter, 1970.

Index